NOT A WORD OF A LIE

NOT A WORD OF A LIE

Bridie Quinn-Conroy

TírEolas

Published by Tír Eolas
Newtownlynch, Kinvara, Co. Galway

I.S.B.N. 1 873821 01 8

Cover design: Anne Korff
Typesetting: Johan Hofsteenge
Printed by Colour Books

Contents

Duras

If you look at Duras on a map, the shape of it bears more than a passing resemblance to the flat head of a blacksmith's anvil. And this resemblance grows stronger if you follow the coastline as it winds south-westward or south-eastward until it finally thickens as you join the main Kinvara - Ballyvaughan road at the junction locals call Geata Bán (the "white gate"). In fact, if you use your imagination to trace an image cut-off line just below Nogra, the only village in Duras, you may be struck by the fact that Duras begins to look very like an island. That's not surprising. It is.

Or rather, it was. Early maps of Duras show it quite definitely as an island. Not below Nogra, as we've imagined, but about a mile above it, the incoming tide cut off most of it from the mainland. Then, about 250 years ago, the local landlord, Patrick French, had embankments raised and an ingenious bridge built and the island of Duras ceased to be.

Four miles west of Kinvara, today Duras is a peninsula, poking out into the Bay and lying almost directly opposite Galway City, but almost 18 miles away by road. To the south-west lie the low foothills of the Burren, while off the western shore of Duras is the island of Aughinish, actually part of County Clare, although for obvious geographical reasons, it has old and strong links with its Galway neighbour, to which it is joined by a causeway.

But all those centuries as an island have had their effect. Duras, although long joined to Kinvara as a single parish, has a quite separate and strongly developed sense of identity, taking in everything from local legends, poets and musicians, to the distinctive qualities of Duras hurlers as compared to those hailing from Kinvara.

A story might help. About 15 years ago, a Department of Education official had the temerity to suggest that, economically and in terms of facilities, it would make sense if Duras N.S. merged with Kinvara N.S. The poor man reckoned without the people of Duras. At a large public meeting held at the school under threat, the suggestion was met with scorn and rejected out of hand. Duras is different, and the people like it that way. The school, by the way, is thriving.

The name Duras, in Irish, is "dubh ros", which means the "black point or promontory", referring either to the original thick tree cover that is still evident on the 1839 O.S. map, or the excellent quality of the rich, black soil still cherished by local farmers.

Lewis' Topographical Dictionary of 1837 states that the entire peninsula takes its name from "a small fertile island close to the shore" on which "are the remains of an ancient Friary with a burial ground". The '"fertile island", of course, is now part of the mainland, but an "ancient friary" is still to be seen, a well-preserved late Medieval Church, surrounded by the now-closed local graveyard.

A few fields away is Duras House, now a youth hostel, but once the summer residence of Count de Basterot, in the garden of which Lady Gregory and W.B. Yeats sketched out the idea of a national theatre one summer's afternoon in 1898. Duras touches the wider world at points like these. But they're not why it's the place it is. It's the people who make a place. and it's the people of Duras - friends, neighbours and relations - that Bridie Quinn-Conroy celebrates in these pages.

Foreword

About 15 years ago, I came to live in a thatched house in Duras that was occupied by two old brothers, Tom and Sean Fahy, when Bridie Quinn-Conroy was growing up. Coming, as I did, from Chicago, I was fascinated by the history of Kinvara and Duras, and in 1988 published two small books. One was called "Kinvara History: A Family Affair", and the other, "St. Colman's Church", which dealt with the history of the pre-Emancipation R.C. church that local people were then refurbishing.

Then, in 1992, folklorist Caoilte Breatnach originally from Dublin but settled, like myself, in the area, published "A Word in Your Ear", a selection of folklore from Kinvara and Duras. At this stage, you might have concluded that Kinvara and Duras were well served so far as publications were concerned.

But both Caoilte and I are, in that colourfully expressive term, "blow-ins", and no matter how deeply we might dig in bringing to light aspects of history and folklore, we would always lack something essential that no amount of reading or research could make up for. We were not born here. But Bridie Quinn-Conroy was.

I read the first draft of Bridie's book about 3 years ago and I recognised at once that here was the "missing dimension" that did not simply complement but enriched with a wealth of detail and personal experience the efforts of "blow-ins" like myself. In "Not a Word of a Lie", you are introduced to the "inner history" of Duras, the story of particular men and women, their struggles and joys, their sorrows and small, but important, triumphs, in a way that documents or parish records can, at best, only hint at.

But this is not simply another contribution to the growing number of books on local history. In these pages you will meet a distinctive community, made up of real people, of a kind that once was typical of the rural West of Ireland and to a certain degree, is typical still, though fast disappearing. It's also the story of a young woman growing up and eventually leaving that community and this too reflects what was, and still is, a common pattern in the West of Ireland. So that too gives this book a broader context, one that many people of Bridie's generation, who come from a similar sort of background, will readily identify with.

"Not a Word of a Lie" is written with warmth and affection, as well as a clear-eyed awareness that the "good old days" were not always what they are sometimes nostalgically cracked up to be. I've certainly enjoyed reading it and think you will too.

Now I've said enough. Let's turn the page and listen to what Bridie has to tell us.

Jeff O'Connell

As it was in the beginning

Home for me was a three bedroomed single storied thatched house, the only house at that time, built on the brand iron. This was a triangular piece of land owned by my father and Tommy Kilkelly, Crushoa, on which there was no other dwelling. It was mandatory that the house should be thatched every 5 years or so, with barley or wheaten straw. In one way, the thatch acted as a type of central heating and again as a type of cooling system. In winter the house was warm and cosy with turf fires blazing inside, and the thatch keeping the heat in. In summer the thatch kept the house cool by not allowing the heat of the sun in.

When the golden crown of thatch was in place, and the last hazel rod well set, then it was time to white wash. It was always considered a woman's job and was done on a fine sunny day. White wash was lime mixed with water and well stirred. Then it was brushed on and left to dry. Next day a second coat was put on and then it looked as white as snow and as fresh as a daisy. Sometimes the bean an tí put in some Recketts Blue and the result was an indigo colour which it was thought lasted longer than lime alone.

Our kitchen was big and had two windows but no back door. The fireplace was wide with a large arch built all around it. There was a hook to hold the kettle or pot. To the right of the fire was an ashpit, over which was built a stone hob. Every morning the ashes were taken out in an ash can, but in an emergency you could sweep it into the ashpit under the hob until later. With the warm ashes

13

under it, naturally the hob got very hot so we usually kept a cushion on it. But once when Tom Fahy sat on it - bare stone with no cushion - he immediately jumped up and shouted: "'Pon my word that's hotter than the hob of hell"! On a cold winter's night with snow on the ground, that's when the hob became a favourite hotspot. Opposite it on the left hand side of the fire was a big strong timber box painted the same colour as the arch. It lay on its side and into it was packed enough of sods to keep the fire burning for the night.

We had a half door or a door and a half. The half door was used to keep out any fowl who might be tempted to step inside in search of food. It was also used to keep in any young toddlers who might be tempted to step outside to explore the big bad world. It could also be used to keep in the heat while at the same time allowing ventilation, and fresh currents of air to flow in over the half door. And finally, but not for us, it was a great support for the grandfather or grandmother who might like to rest their elbows on it, while gazing in peace and comfort at the goings on outside. Cats loved the half door and perched on it often, thereby having an equally good view both inside and outside. When somebody was leaving the kitchen, the usual request was "Pull out the half door after you . . ."

There were no carpets on our bedroom floors but there were throw rugs beside the beds. Getting ready for bed on a cold winter's night meant that a lot of agile skipping and hopping was done to make sure that your bare feet never touched the stone floors. There was a boarded or timber floor in the parlour and it was always shiny and polished. There was a fireplace in which a fire was lit from November to March so that we could do our lessons in peace, especially on nights when everybody in the village decided to come on "cuairt" to our house. There hung a large bevelled mirror over the fireplace and we loved to preen in front of it before going anywhere. Against the far wall was a sideboard with all of my mother's knick knacks on it - glasses, eggstands, a teapot, an unusual butter dish, and a lovely tray brought from Pebble Beach. In the drawers she kept her white-handled cutlery. Directly beside the sideboard hung an old fashioned clock, not a grandfather one, but a fine specimen which still lives to tell the time. In the middle of the floor was a round table with two leaves which could be put up or let down. A white tablecloth nearly always covered this table and once, when my father decided to give away our dog, Freckles, my sister Julia and I hid with the dog under the table cloth for hours, before finally being found. The room was very big and there was a huge wardrobe against the far wall, into which you could step and be hidden, and I often did. During the summer, a big double bed was put into the room, making provision for another family, the Dalys, who came on holidays every summer. One armchair and four dining room chairs completed the parlour furniture and made it the most pleasant room in the house.

So this was the home into which we were born, and in which we lived until it was time to move on. This was the home built a hundred years before, even, it was said, long before the road was made. This was the home over which my parents presided, and of which they were so proud. It was a friendly place, with certain rules to be kept and every occupant had to pull its weight once old enough.

My father, Michael Quinn, was born into a family of six children, two boys, John and Michael, and four girls, Maire, Kate, Bridget and Margaret. When he was only 4 years of age his father died, and his mother had an uphill struggle trying to rear them on her own. When he was 5 years of age, his mother stood him up on a stool and taught him how to tackle the horse. His brother, John, evinced no interest whatsoever in the farm or in the work attached to it so, as a result, much depended on Michael from a very early age. That being the case, my poor father had an extensive working life, starting when he was a young lad of 5 years and only ending with his death at the ripe old age of 91. John ran off to America on the same day as Tom Fahy, Parkmore, and never again returned to Duras - all he ever wanted to do was shake the dust of the area off his feet, and this he succeeded in doing in style. Kate also emigrated to America, became Mrs King and never saw her native place again. She was a great melodeon player and many years ago, Jim Droney, the famous concertina player and father of Chris Droney, told me that he used to play with her at the local hooleys, and he had this to say - "She was a very handsome woman, and fellows used to come from the four parishes, not alone to see her, but also to hear her music". In 1967, when I visited her in her home in New York for her 80th birthday, her piece de resistance was to play the Stack of Barley on the melodeon, while dancing with her son, Pat, and holding the melodeon behind his back - with her arms right round him. Even at that age she was note and step perfect. My father's sister, Maire, married Bartley Faherty who owned a public house in Knock, Spiddal, and reared a large family of whom Jimmy is still hale and hearty and a true Irish wit. One of the girls was called Frances and she was bridesmaid for my parents' wedding. She later went off to Christchurch in New Zealand, married and became Mrs Connaghton - never to set foot in Ireland again. Another of my father's sisters, Bridget, got married locally to Michael Carty, and died while giving birth to twins. Margaret lived in Galway where she remained a spinster. And so they all moved out and gave my father a chance to look out for himself. He married rather late in life but my mother was well worth waiting for, as she was such a marvellous person. She was born Julia Folan in Knock, Spiddal, into a large family of eight children - five boys, John, Martin, Steve, Ned and Mike, and three girls, Mary, Julia and Nora. They were a poor family and the young people all emigrated to America two by two. Mary and John went first and then sent for Ned and Mike. After a year, Martin and Julia joined them and, finally, Steve and Nora. America was all the richer for all of these wonderful young people having worked there, and Ireland all the poorer. While my mother was away, her father, Steve, wrote her a letter and she kept it and showed it to me when I reached the use of reason. It was written in most beautiful handwriting and was heartbreaking in content:

"My dearest daughter, Julie," it said, "Every night as I say my prayers, I ask the good Lord to look after ye all. I wonder will I ever see your lovely face again? I regret very much the circumstances that made my own flesh and blood leave the homeland shores forever. At times like this, I thank God that your poor mother did not live to see an empty nest - empty and lonely. Stay true to your religion, dear daughter, and write often to your old dad - Steve."

I thought it was a most heartbreaking letter, but very well written and very well put together. "Grandfather Steve must have been a well-educated man", I said to my mother. "Self taught" she said, "and very well read. Whenever and wherever he could lay his hands on a book, he did so, and before he left it aside he could recite pages of it off by heart".

Often in later years, I longed for his retentive memory when I was struggling with Shakespeare or Wordsworth.

When their mother died and their father became ill, the eight Folan young people met in Martin's home at 48 Maple Street, Norwood, Mass. to decide which of them would return to look after him. Steve opted to come back, which he did, subsequently married and reared a lovely family of my first cousins. Mary, my mother's eldest sister, also returned home some years later, became Mrs Keady and lived in Park, Spiddal. Nora, the youngest sister, died as a result of peritonitis and is buried in Calvary cemetery outside Norwood. Julia, my mother, came home to spend a short holiday in Knock, met and married my father and came to live in Duras. She had travelled extensively while in America, having actually been in 47 out of the then 48 states. She used to say that she suffered from wanderlust, but never missed any of it once she settled down. She could turn her hand to anything, and was the lady who introduced the lemon meringue and the angel cake to the village menu. People turned to her when troubled or distressed as she was a good listener, and was then a woman of action rather than words. "A great woman who lived for her family", was how Patrick Connors from Trácht described her recently, "A great woman altogether".

Politics played an important part in my father's life. He was a Fianna Fail fanatic. He condemned all other parties and policies and would not discuss them with us, but that didn't deter us from delving into the mysteries of others, and we selected our own parties rather than be driven to choose them. He was the delegate to the Comhairle Ceantair meetings or the Conventions, usually held in

Ennis. He cycled there and back, a slight man on a bicycle, with a hat pulled low over his forehead, and bicycle clips keeping his trousers from becoming entangled in the gear-case or chain. He was a personal friend of Robbie Lahiffe, Gort, and loved to meet him at the fair. He also knew Gerald Bartley, another T.D. from Connemara, and they met in Galway several times to discuss the plight of the West, or so my father liked to think. His greatest claim to fame was the moment when, after a convention in Ennis, Eamonn De Valera crossed down over the benches to my father, shook his hand, and their chat lasted for half an hour. "I'm Eamonn," he was supposed to have said, "I see you at all the conventions. Who are you?" At which my father answered, "I'm Michael Quinn from Duras and I'm a great follower of your party, Fianna Fail". And Eamonn is reputed to have said "Well, I'm very glad to meet you and it's the likes of you makes our party as solid as it is". When election time came round, the job of Presiding Officer in the Duras school polling booth was always given to Michael Quinn and the Clerkship to Pake Curtin and I admit that no more meticulous men could be found.

My father was what would nowadays be called a folklorist with a fund of songs, stories and history. While he lived, he was the local historian, but after his death, the mantle, which he had worn with such credit, was passed on to Páraic Ó hEidhin or Patrick Hynes. In his own inimitable fashion, Páraic revelled in the role and could recite every word of the poems, "Matt Mahon" and "Neptune Vale", unfalteringly. And when it came to an Irish word for which we wanted a meaning, we looked no further than Páraic whom we jokingly called the walking dictionary. In turn, when he passed away, the title passed on to Pat Keane of Aughinish, a folklorist, storyteller and historian, as well as a musician and prize-winning sean-nos singer.

Lots of folklore collectors came to our house to record lore for posterity. One evening, I raced in from school and beheld a man sitting in the kitchen with a "yoke" in front of him and my father telling a story into it. I backed up and sat down on a chair, only to rise again quickly, as I had sat on the visitor's hat, something which I was never allowed to forget. That man was Ciarán Bairéad, the first of many collectors. He was followed by Sean Mac Reamoinn, Leo Corduff and, in later years, Ciarán Mac Mathúna. The collected folklore is safely kept in the archives in University College Dublin and, hopefully, in years to come, it will be of some benefit to his great great grandchildren.

Seán Keane from Caheravoneen, Kinvara, told me recently that he was at a concert once in Kinvara Boys School, organised by Joe Muldoon, the principal. My father was the second item on the programme, he said, and he brought the house down. "What was he doing?", I asked. "Sitting on a chair", said Seán, "with Mary standing on his right playing the violin, Nora standing on his left and you and Julia sitting on his knees. He sang three songs", said Sean, "and then he put ye all to one side and Mary played a jig and he danced". "And where was my mother?" I asked. "Down in the audience; waiting to walk ye all home", he said, "and your father cycled". It's something I don't remember, but it's a memory I'm very glad to hear about.

It's funny the things one remembers about one's parents, and the satisfaction got from remembering. Both Michael and Julia Quinn were very generous people. God knows they hadn't much but what they had, they were willing to share. Once I came home from school, satchel on my back, sandshoes tied around my neck, barefeet pounding as I ran out of the boreen, onto the road, and stopped dead in my tracks. I came face to face with a man driving one of our two cows off up the road. I raced home breathless to tell my father that somebody was stealing our cow, "and if you hurry, you'll catch him around the Mount or the Cross of Nogra". As he had a habit of doing, my father pounded the ground with his right boot, and shook his fist at me. "Sssh and be quiet", he hissed "and don't let anybody hear you. I'm just after lending the cow to that man, because his own cow is dry, and his new baby is only three weeks old. So shut up about stealing the cow and go and do your jobs, I don't want to hear another word about it". I stood looking at him with my mouth open as he walked away. Suddenly, he turned back and shouted, "And make sure that you don't go telling anybody either". I marvelled at this hidden quality of generosity and 'tlaithiúlacht' which nobody was ever to hear about because anonymity was what he craved.

When my eldest sister, Mary, was making her first Holy Communion, she got a new pair of black patent "hornpipe" shoes with lovely silver buckles and white ankle socks. The night before the big day, my mother found out that another little girl in the village had no shoes, so she gave her Mary's new shoes and polished up the old ones for Mary. By doing this, she earned the undying gratitude of that little girl, who managed to be with her when she died and who, to this day, tells the story and prays for her.

Many people remember my father as being cross, cranky, strict and dour. Of course, he was, but so were most fathers of that time. I don't remember seeing any of them playing football with their children, or rocking and rolling with them. They didn't have any spare time and, furthermore, they were much older than the average dads nowadays. But I got on quite well with mine and whenever he got an inclination to slap me with his hat, I backed away and laughed. Several times I caught him looking and smiling as if to say, this one is a survivor, and right here I must tell the ladder incident. Our ladder was old and dangerous with one or two 'bacadaigh' shaky rungs tied with ropes, only waiting for a chance to kill somebody. After serious discussion with my mother, my father ordered a new one, and it was delivered a few days later from Kinvara on the back of a lorry. There was much shoving, pushing, lifting and sidestepping as it was unloaded. There it lay, creamy-beige, smooth to the touch, and safe. Next evening, when I came home from school, I discovered that Seán Fahy, the thatcher from Newtownlynch, was thatching the rick of hay in the haggard, and was using the new ladder. At 4 o'clock my father, who was handing up scallops or hazel rods and generally fussing around the base of the ladder, went into the kitchen with Seán for tea and currant cake. I seized my chance and out I went. I looked up at the ladder, as it lay against the rick, its top almost reaching into the sky, or so it seemed to me. I climbed cautiously and slowly step by step, rung by rung, and I got a heady, exhilarating, feeling. Two more steps and I could jump on to the hay, and look out over the whole countryside.

Alas! That was not to be. My father, who seemed to have eyes in the back of his head, had seen me leaving the kitchen and, with some sixth sense, had followed me. Now he had just spotted me on my high perch and instead of coaxing me down, he roared like a bull at the top of his voice, "Come down before you get killed". Rather than descend properly, and get the wallop I so richly deserved, I jumped and fell to the ground on a heap of straw. The ladder jumped too, but was not as lucky as I was. It bounced off the hay and, off balance, crashed into the double stone wall of the cabbage garden. The three top rungs broke off and fell into the cabbage, and the rest of it hopped on to the ground in the haggard. In hindsight, this doesn't say much for the workmanship of the ladder, does it? My father, small blame to him, went berserk. He danced a jig, or rather leaped into the air and performed some great footwork on the way down. He shook both fists at me, like a conductor conducting his orchestra. All the time, he was getting very red in the face, and with all the jumping, didn't his hat fly off. "You are a limb of the devil", he roared, and I didn't wait to ask "Which limb?" So, before he got his second breath, I turned, made for the gap and leaped into the next field. I spent an hour hiding in the orchard behind the apple trees. When my stomach began to talk to my backbone with the hunger, I plucked up my courage and walked into the kitchen. My father sat, as usual, directly under the hanging lamp, reading the Irish Press. Just as I passed him, he pounced and caught my arm. "You could have been killed", he said in a loud voice, with his glasses dangling and the paper bunched up in his fist. "You could have been killed", he repeated. Tearfully and really sorry, I said "I'm sorry about the ladder..." whereupon he interrupted me and said "Never mind the ladder, sure it was too long anyhow. A ladder can be replaced but a child cannot". So ended the ladder episode, which taught me one lesson which I had already guessed, but which I now knew for sure, the deep love and protective feelings a parent has for his children, even the most destructive ones.

21

My mother was a very intelligent and cultured woman. She laid great emphasis on reading and on lengthy discussions. She had seen certain things firsthand, at which Duras people could only guess. Her theory was that everybody should be allowed to give an opinion, and she believed that rules and regulations should be made to suit many, rather than the few. She taught Irish conversation in Seamount College for years, walking in 3 miles every Sunday, teaching for 3 to 4 hours and walking home again. The Superioress, Mother Ignatius O'Connell, and herself became firm friends, especially when the school was raised to Class A standard, as the students slowly but surely became bilingual. We ourselves could move from Irish to English as easily as my mother, and this fluency was of great benefit to us in oral examinations, also in written ones, later in life.

Social occasions when both of my parents went out together were very, very rare. Shortly after getting married they went to a dance which was held in the old "Big House", the ruins of which are still visible behind The Traveller's Inn in Nogra. Dancing was going ahead nicely when, all of a sudden, didn't the parish priest rush in, wielding a big 'camóg'. He had abandoned his pony and trap up the road near Brans' house, and had walked the last half mile so his attack was totally unexpected, and his presence put the fear of God in the dancers. He struck out left, right and centre, knocking some, and sending the majority running for cover into the garden, ploughing through the shrubs, the flowers, anywhere just to hide from the priestly wrath. He promised them eternal burning in hell's fire. He promised disclosure of their names from the altar, for disobeying the rules as he had laid them down. There should be no dancing for it was an immediate occasion of sin. He frightened them so badly that some of them lived in perpetual fear of losing their immortal souls, and I doubt if they ever danced again.

When my father was a young man of 20, himself and Tom Linnane, Nogra, used to pal around together. Well, one year they decided to save some money so that when the time came to go to the Galway races they would be ready. To do this, they painstakingly saved pennies and tuppences, and after a long time, they had saved half a crown each. They went to Farrell's shop and changed the pennies into a silver half a crown each. My father tied his half crown in a piece of sacking and hid it in a rafter in the henhouse. This was a small shed with a rather unpleasant smell so the money was safe enough, as nobody would ever think of searching it, for money, anyhow. Tom also tied his money into a piece of sacking, and hid it in a rafter in the pigs' sty.

Race morning dawned fine and sunny. The pair of boyos had arranged to leave home early, so eight o'clock found my father bright-eyed and bushy tailed, stealing into the shed and retrieving his precious half crown. He stuffed it into his pocket and made straight for Linnanes. But, on reaching the Cross of Nogra, he got a terrible feeling that all was not well.

Tom was sitting sadly on the small wall which surrounded the sty, and his face was as long as a wet Sunday.

"Are you ready?" asked my father.

"Aw no", said Tom. "It means that I cannot go now until the piggy-bank opens". It seems that the money had fallen from the rafter into the pigs' trough, and the sow had eaten it, and now Tom was waiting for the sow to go to the toilet and pass the money. In due course, the bank did open, the money was found and the lads had a great time.

I'm told that my father was a great hurler and never played in the same position during the course of a match. He could put in a goal, and race to the other end of the pitch to receive the puck out. His two playing cronies were John Joe Reidy and Tommy Sullivan (Maher). The story was that opposing teams used to pray that one or other of them would get a whack of a hurley and become incapacitated for a match or two. My father's nephew, Jim Faherty from Knock, told me that before a hurling match, a long time could be spent stitching the sliotar, which was just a ball of cork covered with a strip of leather. Sometimes, it was the tongue of an old boot stitched with wool thread and Jim said that there was great hullaballoo once, when the ball of cork went into the net, for a goal and the leather strip went over the bar for a point. Míle murder on the field and much scratching of heads. "Now where was the sliotar, in the goal or over the bar?" Not a present day dilemma anyhow.

I hope nobody thinks that my father was a paragon of virtue. He could be as cranky as a briar, or as short tempered as could be. He was mad about work and couldn't understand how anybody could sit down idly. He was intolerant of laziness and said that things done badly were totally unacceptable. "Creep down", he would screech at me when we were sowing slits "and don't be gathering bad mind standing up". He was as hard on his family as he was on himself. He was a very strict father who kept our noses to the grindstone - except the rebellious ones. He was squeamish about injections or being hurt and he could never kill a pig or even a hen. He expected to be waited on at home; for example, his dinner was always put out first, his fresh underwear and shirts were always left on the back of a chair before the fire and nobody ever read the paper before he did.

Only once did I really clash with my father, and I mean really clash. I thought he was making the greatest mistake of his life and about to ruin mine. I was about 14 years of age and I answered an advertisement in the Irish Press which said: "Wanted by Travelling Show: young girl who can sing and dance. Apply to William A. Costello, c/o Box No." As I could dance a jig and sing a song, I thought I would be the perfect choice. I wrote and waited for an answer, never doubting for one moment but that one would come. It did, and the morning the postman handed me the brown envelope addressed to Bridie Quinn I was transported with joy, and already had visions of tripping the light fantastic across the stage in some far off city. When I read the short missive, I discovered that William A. Costello had asked me to come to Dublin for an interview. But how in God's name would I tell my parents, get money and present myself properly? So two nights later, I cajoled my father into reading the sheet of paper, and he almost hit the roof. How dare I bring the family into disrepute? How dare I try to make an idiot of myself, for fear I wasn't bad enough already? He went on and on, ranting and raving, and point blank refusing either permission or money. I was utterly devastated, sure that my father had blighted a wonderful showbiz career, and sure that I'd never forgive him, when a few days later, he said in a taunting manner: "I'm sure Willie Costello will be down himself soon, to see what has happened to you". Of course, by the time I was 16 years of age, I understood that in his wisdom he knew that I wasn't in the slightest way qualified for the job. But shortly afterwards we renewed our friendship, and sometime later, we discussed my near brush with the stage. "You know Bridie", he said, "even though you got an interview, it doesn't mean that you'd have got the job, so I only saved you a lot of heartbreak." Again, the protective feeling of a parent for its offspring when the first tentative shaky steps are being taken from childhood to adulthood. Perhaps he should have let me try anyhow!

These, then, were my parents who loomed so large in my life. My father, strict, small of stature, but with a huge generous heart and great physical strength. My mother, tall, with a wealth of hair held in a bun, and a gold watch on a black velvet band around her neck. My father who wouldn't waste a piece of straw, let alone a second of time. My mother who loved to remind us there were endless places in the world worth visiting, and endless places she herself had visited. My father who thought that going to secondary school was a waste of time, because he said all that it does is make all officers and no soldiers, but allowed his mind to be changed by my mother who thought that in all walks of life education is no load. Their lives were lived so humbly, so unpretentiously, so hardworkingly so that the lives of their children would be easier, better, more rewarding and more fulfilling.

I remember them well

L iving as we did in a rural, remote area, we learned to depend on ourselves for almost all necessities, and we learned to depend on our neighbours for a different slant on life, and how it should be lived. The community was small, and, as I remember it now, representative of all walks of life, had I but known it - farmers, teachers, shopkeepers, builders, thatchers, nuns and housewives.

Our nearest neighbours were the Hynes and Sullivan families. I was as much at home in their kitchens as I was in my own. Maggie Hynes and Molly Sullivan, both mothers of large families, had a very strong effect on me, and I can still feel their influence to the present day. They were stalwart workers, and both had traumatic events in their lives. Maggie's husband, Martin, died when he was very young and she was left to rear the family of nine all alone. They were poor but had love and to spare for each other and she made a great job of their rearing. Molly's youngest daughter, Áine, died after a long sickness and she was laid out in her First Holy Communion dress and veil. It had a devastating effect on the whole neighbourhood and was a shattering blow to poor Molly. Yet both of those women smiled a lot, and for the sake of their families, raised themselves above personal sadness, and each managed to present to us all a caring, kind and community involved life. They taught me strength of character and a wonderful ability to smile in the face of adversity.

Nonie Fahy of the local public house was a very charismatic person. She had curly hair, plaited, pulled back and wound round her head or put into a bun. When she worked hard, little ringlets curled around her face and she looked years younger. She was a comfortable sort of person, one on whose shoulder you could cry and I'm sure many people did. She was like a banker because she loaned money, and was the first to offer money when the necessity arose, and I can tell you that it often did. She never refused to give to anybody who needed it, and it was her name which first came to the tongue when an emergency occurred. She was a happy person, even though she, too, had a terrible personal tragedy. Her eldest son, John Joe, had died at about 10 years of age from an ordinary appendix operation which had gone horribly wrong. While I live I'll never forget the shock waves which ran through the congregation when news of his death was read out at Duras Mass on that Sunday so many years ago. Despite this great loss, she always had a cheery smile, and had plenty of time to listen and plenty of advice to give. She helped thousands in distress, and by her example and her availability to others, she taught me caring and kindness. She had a shrewd brain and ran an excellent business which showed me, even then, that women could play a big part in business in a community.

Mike and Mary Farrell ran the local grocery shop and, again, their lives and how they lived them had a permanent effect on me. Their shop stood on its own away from the house and when you knocked at their kitchen door at night one of them got the keys, walked out to the shop door, unlocked it, went in behind the counter, lit a match and then lit an oil lamp with a globe. Finally, they stood there waiting for the order which, to be quite honest, was never of great value.

"Two lbs of sugar, quarter lb of tea, half-quarter of common tobacco and a box of matches", was a usual list. Mr. Farrell was a genial moustached man, who wore a hat, and who chewed little bits of tobacco. He always wore a suit and looked as clean as a new pin. Mary Farrell was a tall lady, who was always as busy as a bee. She was an unpretentious person and told me once that she had no time for the trappings of fame, "Give me my own little corner", she said, "and I'm quite happy". Very often she looked sad, and we, as youngsters, thought it was because she had two daughters who joined the nuns in enclosed orders and could never come home again. Every day of their lives, they helped people, gave groceries on tick and never refused to open the shop, even for one tiny item. I loved going to Farrell's shop because, for certain, a bulls eye or two would be pressed into my hot little fist as I picked up my messages and I'd suck away to my heart's content as I skipped back home. From knowing them and from observing how they lived, I learned patience and honesty. I also was influenced by their humility and their prayerful lives, as once or twice I heard them reciting the rosary as I stood outside about to knock and call them to serve me in the shop.

Another young person who had a great influence on me was Margaret O'Meara. She stayed in our house and helped my mother as we children came along. We called her Mago or Gagga, and she was the nicest young person we ever knew. She was always willing to help, and always willing to play games. She never got cross or bad tempered and my mother used to call her "my little treasure". She was never jealous or envious of others and her temperament was placid and even and unruffled. She had a lasting effect on me because I learned cheerfulness, ease and evenness of temper from her, and she had an indestructible faith and thought that through prayer every small problem can be solved and every small crease ironed out. To the present day, she manages to make molehills out of mountains.

During the long winter nights our kitchen seemed a haven for many of the villagers, where they would be sure of a warm seat, a good discussion and tea and currant cake. They made predictions about the rise and fall of prices of beef, spuds, cattle, hay, sheep, pigs, barley, wool or a pint, and were very often right. They talked about the weather and were never satisfied. If it rained, they needed sun badly. When the sun shone, they prayed for rain. They moved on to local gossip; Whose match was made at the last fair? Did Johnny so and so leave any money at all? Was it true that one of the priests said that we'd soon have a mission? Then came the stories about fairies, the 'cóiste bodhar' or headless coach, Jack O' the Lantern, and the 'beansí' and we listened with our mouths open and the hair standing on the tops of our heads, as we shivered with pleasure and with fright as we sat in the comparative safety of the hob with the fire making A.B.C's on our shins.

Doing odd jobs was an accepted part of visiting. They gave hair cuts to young lads, by leaving a plate on top of the head and cutting the hair all around it, not forgetting to leave a "bob" or a few lonely ribs hanging down the forehead. Next day, the youngsters looked like criminals with the bare stubbly hair cut and the short bob. They also mended bicycles, fixed punctures, or re-stitched tyre wires with packing needles and woollen thread. They mended shoes or boots, stiched on 'taoibhíns' or sidepatches, put on new toecaps, soles or half soles. They hammered on protectors or studs on the heels and soles to give extra life and prevent them from wearing down too quickly.

Two of the visitors who came on 'cuairt' to our house were Martin Mooney and Peter Bohannon, and both had a tangible influence on me when I was growing up. Martin was a builder and the man whom most people would remember because he built a lot of houses inside Geata Bán, and renovated as many more. "My monuments", he used to call them. He was very clever and very well read. He told me the story of the Graf Spee, the German battleship which was scuttled in 1939. He could repeat every line of Samuel Taylor Coleridge's Rime of the Ancient Mariner, and often regretted that there wasn't more of it. He could repeat what he had read in the newspaper, word for word, even though he had read it three months previously. He had his own ideas about things and the first time he heard two singers singing in harmony he said, "It was a pity they didn't sing the same song". Pete was equally as clever as Martin. He was a farmer and should have been a jeweller, or even an inventor. There wasn't anything he couldn't do with his hands. He could spread out a sheet of paper, take a watch or clock apart, clean and oil all of the pieces while all the time threatening us not to cough in case we scattered them, and then reassemble them in perfect working order. But his love lay with maths. He could add, subtract, divide and multiply thousands mentally. No sum was too hard, and I remember that when my sister, Mary, went to Seamount College first, Pete would always take the maths book to read, and his usual comment was, "God knows but I'd have the book done in a couple of nights and I wouldn't want pencil or paper either". They both had infinite patience and from them I learned that "If anything is worth doing at all, it's worth doing well". They worked with precision and great detail, and were always eager to help, and pass on any knowledge which they had. They never indulged in backbiting or gossiping, but preferred to discuss the state of the country, and what life held in store for us all. If they went to visit in one house and heard something juicy, they'd never repeat it in another house, their motto being "Life is too short for tattling".

To supplement the family income, my mother took in a wonderful family for three weeks holidays every summer. They were the Dalys from Ballygaddy House, Ballygaddy Road, Tuam - which to us in our limited little village, was as far away as America. There were five children - George, Kathleen, Eileen, Eithne and Marcus. Their father was a rancher, they had a name on their house and they had a car - three assets which set them apart from ourselves and everybody else we knew. Seeing that they stayed in our house raised us up in the local estimation and so we basked in their reflected glory. When George arrived the first year, the fact that we had no brother of our own, didn't inhibit us in the slightest, and we quickly adopted him; and for three weeks, he was our brother, bossed and threatened and spoiled and scolded as the humour took us. Once I took my father's bicycle for a spin and wouldn't you know, got a puncture. Worse still, I didn't even mention it, so when my father had to go somewhere in a hurry and found the flat bike, he immediately came looking for me – "Where is she?" type of thing, "I'll kill her". But George courageously stepped forward and said, "I did it", whereupon my father backed off and said, "Isn't it little you had to do? And don't let me see you near my bicycle again, or I'll give you a taste of this on the backside" - and he waved the stick and we all fled. I think I fell in love with George at that moment, and the euphoria lasted until he beat me in a race two days later and taunted me, saying "you are as slow as a snail". I quickly fell out of love! Their advent brought a whiff of excitement and interest to the locality every year, and it brought home to us the fact that our village was only a tiny dot in the scheme of things and that they lived a completely different lifestyle. I actually felt serious pangs of jealousy the first time I saw the girls' clothes, lovely dresses, blouses, skirts and a Sunday blazer each. But the girls were so nice and so unspoilt that we settled down and had a great time. Having this family living with us taught us a lot, and it had lifelong effects on us. We learned how to live with others, how to share, how to make others happy and how, above all, not to value worldly goods too much. The family couldn't care less even if we hadn't a lot - we were best friends and went around one for all and all for one. I have very happy memories of that family and how well they adapted to our lifestyle in the heart of the country.

And, finally, the influence my teachers, Mr Moylan and Miss Farrell, had on me as a child has remained with me to this day. They projected images which were indelibly marked into my brain, images which built up self-worth, self-confidence, and self-esteem. Their motto was you can do it, and I found I could. Their motto was try again, and then you'll succeed. Their motto was smile and the world smiles with you. They taught me dedication and reliability.

Undoubtedly, I owe my parents a lot, as I owe my neighbours, Margaret, our visitors, the Daly family and my teachers. I have tried to instil into my life the kindness, patience, tolerance, honesty, shrewdness and certain ethical values which I learned from them as I grew from babyhood into my formative years, and I thank each and every one of them for helping me in various ways to reach my full potential.

Growing up brotherless

L ife in our family followed the normal routine of the country farmer, only a little more difficult, as we were all girls, Mary, Nora, Bridie and Julia, in that order. I'm sure my father would have welcomed a son so he would have help on the farm, as well as an heir to inherit the land. But he never showed any disappointment before us at the absence of a "lad", but appeared quite content with what he had, and settled down to make the most of it, or rather of us. Once I heard him saying to Thomas Mooney, "Sure if I had a son of my own, I'd have to take what I got, even if he were a 'leibide' or fool. Now I'll have the pick of the parish or indeed of the four parishes, for sons-in-law".

For our part, this absence of a brother, or brothers, affected us in several ways, none of which was very important. Indeed to be quite honest, when we saw some of the wimps and sissies and excuses other girls had as brothers, we were quite pleased not to be burdened with anything remotely like them. On the other hand, some girls had smashing handsome brothers - we wouldn't have minded that at all!! In our minds, a brother should be tall, strong and goodlooking; if not, we were just as well off without one. Anything less would not have suited at all.

So it came to pass, that we had no big brother to fight our school battles for us, or frighten away the playground bully. We had to do our own fighting and our own scaring. We punched and shoved and walloped when necessary. In any way we could, we defended our "territorial" rights, and became very good at this defence, developing along the way independence and acute survival instincts. I actually enjoyed the rows and arguments which occurred in the playground or on the road home. Once a tall bony fellow hit my younger sister and I retaliated and struck him - right on the nose. I'm sure Cassius Clay would have been proud of my unerring punch! I felt very protective and strong while I was making contact - but afterwards I ran, and kept out of "Bony's" way for a day or two - the coward's way out. Who needed a big brother anyhow, when we got such satisfaction out of a "bloody" row? Either we were bloodied or else the enemy was. Often my poor mother despaired when she saw me - dishevelled, mucky but triumphant.

However, having no brother made a great difference on the farm. We girls had to help our father doing the jobs which would normally be reserved for boys. These jobs could be anything from sowing slits, picking potatoes, thinning and pulling beet, binding corn, or saving hay - all back breaking and very tiring tasks. These jobs suited lads, but they didn't suit girls. But that didn't deter us from tackling them, and nearly always doing them to perfection.

Each one of us had to turn her hands to these jobs. The minute you came in from school, you had to "get on with it" - because in my father's opinion, "the devil finds work for idle hands", so he made sure that our hands were never idle. So it was, in reality, that even though, or probably because, we were brotherless, we girls were initiated into all aspects of farm chores, and were widely viewed by young farmers of marriageable age as "good catches". We did the farmwork all right, but that doesn't mean we enjoyed it very much.

We had no big brother to take us to the village bonfires, or as we grew older, to the hooleys or Ceílís. We certainly missed out a little there. In the early days my father escorted us, but this proved to be so unexciting for us, and we made it so awkward for him that it soon ceased altogether. Just when you'd be starting to enjoy yourself, my father would jump up as if he had sat on a red hot poker and announce, in a very determined voice - "Time to go home" - and home we'd have to go. So we were delighted when my father told us that we needn't depend on him in future to accompany us to local do's, because he said, "Ye are well able to look after yourselves - ye don't need a father or a brother". This was a great compliment coming from my father and one which we made sure he never regretted paying us.

When young girls had a "crush" on a fellow, they usually danced and clowned around chanting this ditty, "All good girls love their brothers, but I so good have grown, I love another girl's brother far better than my own". This poem, however, was not for us.

Not to be outwitted we altered it and the repeated it to our hearts' content - "All good girls love their brothers, but I alas have none, I love another girl's brother and want him for my own." Thus we changed things to suit ourselves, and suited ourselves when we changed things.

In Duras, where I grew up, in most homes the son was looked on as "the maicín bán" or white haired boy. He got the best of everything, the most of everything, and got it before everybody else. Excuses were made when he did anything wrong, - sure wasn't he a boy and boys will be boys. But in our family, we did not suffer from the "maicín bán" syndrome. There were no favourites and no pets. Consequently, things were distributed rather evenly among us girls - whether it was work, or blame or praise, not forgetting love.

Because we were all girls, this had a dire effect on the clothes issue. When my sister, Mary, who was the eldest daughter, got a new dress, sometimes it was bought, or came in a parcel from America, or was made by my mother. When she had grown out of it, then it was passed on to Nora. By the time it reached me, because I had shot up suddenly like an overgrown mushroom, it was miles too short usually. So a piece had to be inserted in the middle, which I really and truly detested above every other evil. There I was wearing a hand me down, with no hope of ever getting anything new of my own. However, very often God smiled on me and a battered parcel arrived from America, with one or two dresses just my length, and I was transported with joy. Had a brother been between the girls, I always felt that the hand-me-downs would never have reached me. I wonder?

Having no brother, however, meant that we didn't really have any standards by which to measure a young man, although I admit we weren't short of ideas. As well as that, my mother who had five brothers - John, Ned, Mike, Martin and Steve - could, and did, fill us in on manly requirements, and didn't forget to inform us also about manly weaknesses. Nevertheless, we had to act independently, and set up our own standards, and use our own judgement when choosing other girls' brothers. We learned how to look out for each other, and in the heel of the hunt, let it be said that, although growing up brotherless gave us a few minor headaches, I admit that "we never missed what we never had".

Seasonal occupations

Years seemed to pass more slowly than they do now. From one birthday to another loomed long and lengthy. From one Christmas to the next, seemed much longer than one year. However, each month elapsed, and seasonal events took place and occupations continued and life was lived for many and ended for others. Weeks passed into months, and months into years and the rhythm of life became more finely tuned and certain happenings occurred and reoccurred and left memories pleasant and startlingly vivid and, sometimes, disappointing.

Down the road from our house on the brand iron were some fields belonging to a man called Tommy Kilkelly. Being a meticulous farmer, he rotated the crops annually, so the three fields each grew hay, or potatoes or a grain crop like oats, wheat or barley. A family of corncrakes knew this and came to visit the cornfield year in, year out. My father used to say that you could set the clock by them. Several times, I actually heard three corncrakes craking together. As children, we visualised the corncrake as a small brown bird who was slightly silly as he lay on the ground, on his back, with his four legs pointing upwards, keeping up the world, or so he thought. His repeated call was "Look at me, look at me, look at me", and when we heard him, whether we were bringing home the cows, or running home from school, or just playing in the fields, we immediately stood still to listen. We were always under the, perhaps mistaken, impression that the slightest noise could put him off his stride. I'm not sure how we concocted these ideas, but we firmly believed

36

them and listened for, and to, the corncrakes as they returned year after year. They craked every day during the summer months. Now they have become practically silent. I haven't heard a corncrake for years. Most of their natural habitats and environment, which they knew and needed, have disappeared due to land reclamation and the felling of trees and hedges. In reality, the poor corncrake has been evicted. And we are the poorer for his going.

Travelling shows visited Duras, even though it was a remote western coastal area and "out of the beaten track". They came once a year, occasionally twice. Weeks beforehand, a poster was put up on a barn door in Nogra, and we hung around it like bees around honey, or midges around a "cock-bó". We read that William Costello, or Jimmy Stone or, much later, McFaddens, would visit in three weeks time. We whooped with delight in anticipation of this great and much-looked-forward-to event. This intrusion of the outside world into our private lives, was like a breeze from another planet. We were so dependent on ourselves - family, locals and neighbours - for any kind of entertainment, that we regarded it as a miracle to have a travelling show here in the village, to show us exactly what the outside world was like.

Dreams at that time were centred around the impending show. Would we be let? Would there be any money". Needless to say, the children were not always allowed to go, but I remember going once with my father. A small tent had been erected at the cross of Nogra and benches were placed as seating arrangements. That night all steps led to the tent. The men were smoking pipes or Woodbines; the children were sitting expectantly in the front, their eyes "standing in their heads", their cheeks bulging with one or two bull's eyes. The posters had promised songs, magic, tricks, and a short play or two like "Murder by Candlelight" or "East Lynne". Up in front, the tiny stage was shrouded in mystery, partly because the curtains were pulled across and hid everything from view, and partly because of the smoky atmosphere. It was most dramatic and spell-binding. Sitting on the hard seat, my feet firmly planted on the soft grass, my hands sweating in anticipation, surrounded by locals, I thought I was the luckiest child alive. The songs were sung loudly and with gusto. The jokes were funny. The magic was "out of this world", and the play was hauntingly sad. I remember thinking - "when I grow up I want to act on a stage like that", - I actually turned around and confided this secret to everybody around - who were too mesmerised to laugh at me.

I remember well one funny incident. A play was performed called "Murder in the Red Barn" and the butler on stage was reading a character reference he had just got from his employer. He stuffed the paper into his hip pocket as he was walking off stage, but unknown to the actor, the paper fell out and fluttered on to the ground. My father jumped up and called after him, "Hey, sir, you lost your character". It caused a great laugh, and afterwards the actor said "I think we may be able to use that remark in the play in future". Quick as a flash, my father said, "If you do, t'will cost you money". Another great laugh and the actor bowed and said "Money is the root of all evil, my good man". Then everybody clapped and cheered, the curtains were drawn and all was over.

Outside they all stood around, some saying to my father, "You should have said this" and others said, "You should have said that", and my father, who thought he had done a great job was stung to reply, "Arra, shut up, I didn't hear you saying anything, you dummy", and so ended the night.

Next morning, the tent had disappeared and nothing was left but crushed and trodden grass, sweet wrappings, Woodbine packets, matches and papers. We always raced around to see if we could find a penny on the ground - but we were never lucky. Those were great days when the small travelling shows came to the tiny scattered country villages, and gave so much pleasure, and generated such excitement, as well as leaving an indelible mark on the minds of children and adults alike.

Each farmer who owned land in Duras bordering the inlet of Galway Bay also owned some shore. On this shore were huge rocks where seaweed gathered. When the tide went out, the rocks were uncovered, and when the tide came in, they were covered again. This shore was divided between the local farmers, and the "divides" were rotated every year. Given time, each farmer travelled over all the divides so there was never any trouble over who owned what. Sometimes, after a rather rough evening, or an unusually high tide, some of the seaweed became loose and was "brought in by the tide". This was called "buail isteach" or "blow in" and it belonged to the farmer on whose "divide" it landed. There it lay, seaweed knee deep, cart loads of it, all ready to be used as fertilizer, without any time or trouble having been spent on it, and the farmer was usually delighted.

However, this only happened once in a while. All other times, the farmer had to go out on the shore and cut the weed himself. The minute the tide turned to go out, the farmer and his wife and helpers went out to the "divide". I remember two of ours were named The Vialeens, and Coiléar. My father picked his way on the flat stones or pathways that have been there for centuries and, indeed, are still there, as I discovered on a recent visit. He carried a "clew" of ropes and a fork or two and a sharp knife. My mother usually carried a basket of food - bread and butter and a bottle of tea. My father laid the ropes on the ground in a very complex pattern, to form the base of the climin, a sort of raft of seaweed. He left them down horizontally and vertically and very, very carefully as his life literally depended on them. Then the cutting and pulling of the seaweed began.

A frond or tuft of seaweed was grabbed in the left hand and its roots were slashed with the shore knife held in the right hand. Then it was thrown in the general direction of the ropes, and when a large pile was ready, my father forked it onto the ropes. The corners were especially strengthened in case the climín "spread". This work went on for some hours, as the work could be done only while the tide was out. A few minutes was spent snatching a cup of tea.

Suddenly everybody noticed that the tide had turned and was creeping stealthily inwards, inch by inch. Then all the workers gathered up baskets, knives and forks and went home as fast as their legs could carry them, in case they'd be caught by the tide. One person remained to tidy up. In our family, it was my father who stayed and finished off the first day's work. He tied up the ropes and put special "running knots" which could easily be opened next day, and then left them lying on top of the heap of seaweed. Again, he usually paid special attention to the corners, making sure that the seaweed was well packed, so that the incoming tide could not loosen it and sweep it away. The next job was to put some heavy stones on top of the climín in order to "drown" it, to keep it under water, until next day, when another day's cutting of seaweed would be added to it.

Then it was time for him to make his way to the land - slipping from stone to stone, and splashing his way through shallow pools. He was usually very wet when he squelched his way home and was often very tired, "so tired", he said once, "that I could sleep standing up".

However, next morning he was up at "cock shout" bright and early, and long before the tide had turned to go out he was hurrying down the road, carrying two wattles or two large poles, which he would use later to push the climín through the water. Once he reached the bank of seaweed, he removed the stones, loosened the running knots and, once again, began the work of cutting, pulling and forking.

When the tide turned that evening, the climín resembled a huge rectangular raft of seaweed, tied securely with strong ropes, and this concoction was expected to float. Only my father stayed with the climín when the tide came in on the second day. Everybody else went home. My father - as indeed all other fathers in the area - usually had a flask of tea and smoked a pipe of tobacco during the long lonely vigil, waiting for the tide to lift the climín off the ground. Then he pushed it with the wattle out into the deep channel, away from the rocks and small islands, and towards the landing place at the bridge. From our vantage point in the haggard, on a summer's evening, we could easily pick out our father coming slowly and laboriously across the water. When he reached a certain point, we took off like bullets and reached the landing spot in time to catch the rope which he threw and then we pulled him in. Several climíns were often pushed across the water altogether, and the men talked to each other, and their voices echoed and re-echoed as they approached land. I often saw six climíns tied up at the bridge together. Next day, the horses and carts were driven down, and the seaweed was carted off and spread as fertiliser in the tilled fields. Martin Hynes, Tom Linnane, Michael Carty, Mick Linnane, Willie Shaughnessy, Denny Hynes, John Connors, Jack Moloney and Thomas Mooney were great climín makers.

The annual visit of the thresher to the haggard was always an event to be remembered. As children, we always hoped and prayed that the machine would come, either in the evening after school, or best of all, on a Saturday. I will always remember with a tinge of sadness the last time, while I was still in National school, that the 'finisher' came to our yard.

Leaving for school that morning we hoped against hope that the work would not be finished before we reached home that evening. There was no delay after school, no looking for birds' nests, no "streeling" along the roads. We raced home as fast as "chain lightening". As we reached Sullivan's hill, the throbbing and drumming of the heavy threshing machine reached us. We stood still to listen, our hearts thumping and, sure enough, we heard it - the loud rolling sound, now faint, now much clearer, vibrating in the air. Straining on tiptoes, we could see a feathery plume of smoke rising high above the trees which grew near our house.

We raced the last few yards, tumbling in our haste and barely waiting to get up. We sped along the dusty road, the bigger ones dragging the smaller ones. The neighbours' children came too, and all together we invaded the already crowded scene. Painted bright red, the threshing machine or "finisher" sat in the haggard like a straining hungry animal. It belched smoke, and it shuddered and shook, while its wide rubber belts sent out a rubbery sickening smell. A "meitheal" or crowd of neighbours swarmed all over the place.

Standing on the stack of corn, Sonny Sullivan had a two-pronged fork on which he impaled a sheaf of corn and sometimes two. He raised the fork and threw the sheaf unerringly on to the platform of the thresher. In the whole evening's work, he only missed the target once. My father was standing on the platform loosening the bands of the sheaves, spreading out the ears and, at the same time, feeding it expertly into the gaping mouth until it vanished into the rumbling, throbbing interior or as it was called - into the drum. He was called the feeder and had an important and dangerous job. He had to keep the machine fed and at the same time, he had to be extra careful as one slip and he, himself, could end up as fodder.

Out in front, Thomas Mooney had the task of doing his best to keep the golden straw forked out of the way. It kept clouding, tumbling out and half hid Thomas and Mattie Quinn at times. They pushed it away and two others, Mick Linnane and Jack Moloney, forked it on to the rick which was being built not too far away. On the side of the machine was a wide, thin slit, out of which rich, thick, golden grain came spilling, tumbling, pouring - forming a cone which made one want to stick one's hands into it and let the grain run refreshingly through one's fingers. Along came Mickey Keane, John Glynn, Patrick Connors and Martin Hynes filling the corn into bags and carrying them into the barn where it was spilled out on the floor, swept clean or sometimes covered with a "bratach" or large piece of sacking. The work continued without any stop until the last sheaf had been threshed.

A slight disturbance took place when Sonny was coming to the bottom of the stack of corn. A family of mice had lodged in the sheaves, and now found themselves being evicted. Some of them ran safely to the wall, but some were not quick enough and the dog, with a killer instinct, always succeeded in committing a few murders. The whole "meitheal" then crowded into the kitchen where extra helpings of bacon and cabbage and tasty floury potatoes were served. Our kitchen table could seat eight people - maybe nine at a pinch - so if there was a big crowd, two sittings would be needed. The older men were fed first and then the 'luifearnach' or younger boyos got a bite. My mother, who was an excellent cook, always made 'cairigin' and jelly for dessert on such an occasion and I can assure you, they were short-lived. Later, much later, they disbanded and went home, forks and rakes on their shoulders, pleased at a job well done.

Twice or three times a year, when the farmer wanted to sell some cattle or sheep, lambs, calves or pigs, he went to a fair in Kinvara. Nowadays fairs are a thing of the past, replaced by the Mart, a highly organised and efficient auction, but not at all as colourful as the fair.

The October fair was the most important one held in Kinvara. The farmer left home at 2 am or 3 at the latest and "walked" the animals to the town, a distance of three miles from Duras and six from Aughinish. Pigs were usually brought in horsecarts, with the standards and carts up and the top covered with sacking or a bratach. On reaching the town, the first thing you noticed was the noise - pure bedlam with men talking, cows lowing, sheep bleating, horses neighing, dogs barking, boys shouting and Seán Saor advertising his wares. Animals were stamping and tails lashing as they stood safely, albeit unwillingly, penned between carts and doors. The streets were filthy - the animals just lifted their tails and left little piles behind. Walls were splashed and dirty, and unless you kept your eyes wide open and skipped agilely around - first to the left and then to the right - you, too, could be splashed and dirty. It was a full time job while walking down the street to avoid whipping tails, kicking legs and "spouting benedictions". The cattle never stood still - shoving, pucking, stamping, pushing, backing and staggering. It was a marvellous symphony of sights and sounds.

Locking the doors in Duras was unheard of when I was growing up. The fear of being robbed, the fear of unwanted visitors was non-existent. You never had to wait for an invitation to visit; nobody ever knocked on the door when coming to call. You just walked in the street to the door, lifted the latch and stepped right in. The smile was always a welcoming one. The greeting was always a hospitable, old fashioned, good-natured Irish one. You could walk the unlit roads in safety. You need never stand on ceremony. It was a lovely old-fashioned easy world, with lovely old-fashioned people, who really didn't want things changed. It was a safe place for us when we were growing up, and even the monotony of seasonal occupations and the sameness of events year in, year out, couldn't mar our enjoyment of life and our delight in things simple and uncomplicated.

To, from and at school

W e walked to and from Duras school every day, a journey of perhaps six miles. To be truthful, we didn't walk; we ran, leaped over walls, climbed over stiles and raced through meadows. We were like quicksilver as our moods changed. We lingered and loitered, walked briskly, ran, galloped, crept like snails and barely moved. We enjoyed good health and were physically very fit. So the thought of a long walk to and from school didn't worry us at all. Actually we looked forward to it every day, as something different happened on each daily journey.

The journey to school differed in many ways from the homeward journey. Even though our mothers got us out early, still we were inclined to "streel" along, losing a few minutes here and a few seconds there, with the result that we had to "race like the dickens" over the last mile or so. The shortest route from our house to the school was up the road, over by the boreen past Poll Phroinsias, out by the Ball Alley or down to Cloosh Road, past Knockaculleen cross, past Curtins, over by the Chapel and into school in Newtownlynch. The children from the main village came by the road as far as the Ball Alley - this was built by the local people so the youngsters could play ball, and was the spot where the boreen and road met. Whichever group - them or us - passed to school first, every morning built a little pile of stones or, as we used to say "a kileen of stones" - an unwritten message saying, "Hurry, we are ahead". The Indians had smoke signals, we had piles of stones. On the homeward journey every evening, we knocked the pile, and rebuilt it next morning. Down near Knockaculleen cross, we often crossed into a field, leaped a few walls, frightened the lives out of peacefully grazing cattle and - out of breath - came out onto the road at The Chapel, thus cutting off a quarter of a mile.

Even though the journey to school was a rapid race against the clock, we still had time to notice many, many beautiful things. We noticed the silvery lacy spiders' webs, woven in and through the briars and bushes, glistening with dew drops in the early morning sun. I remember following the snail's spidery slimy track as it crossed and recrossed the road and immediately "a whiz kid" among us devised a new game. "How many snail's tracks can you find?"

Away we raced.

"I've found one, and another, and another", came the excited cries as we sped ahead, passed each other out, caught up and repassed. Occasionally, we found the snails just on the grassy edge of the road, where they lay "playing dead", until we raced away. There must have been millions of snails taking early morning constitutionals in those days!

Walking along, chattering, repeating poems or tables, suddenly silence descended on us - a lone cyclist had appeared in the distance. This was the master on his way to school. It must be getting late - we had no way of knowing what time it was, as watches were an unknown quantity. We used the sun and the postman to keep us on the straight and narrow, timewise. We tried to make up for lost time by running like hares but as he got closer, we walked sedately. We held our breaths as he reached us and while he passed, because the whole mood of the day was set by what he said as he passed the long line of us in single file. Oh! We had him well taped! If he said "Dia dhaoibh a pháistí" - forecast for a good mood, an easy day, and what harm if the bata or stick is broken! If, however, he said "Brostaígí a pháistí" - this was a different kettle of fish. It spelled out a bad mood, slogging at lessons all day and the inevitable question - "Cé bhris an bata?" Usually, we let him cycle away in silence and the next minute we erupted into noisy chatter - "Give me the answers to the sums!", "Ask me my spellings" or "Do ye think we could pretend we got 10 times tables instead of 12 times?"

"Mitching" from school was a hazard and a challenge which many pupils tried out once, twice and, sometimes, more often. I myself "mitched" once - just to see what it was all about. Funnily though, I didn't mitch because I disliked school or because I hadn't my homework done. Not at all. Actually, I enjoyed going to school and had no reason to try to escape it. I just strayed off to see exactly what was the appeal of "mitching".

Anyhow, that particular morning, near the chapel, I told my sister that I needed to shake some sand out of my shoe, and she and the others should run on ahead as we were already late. This they did and the minute I got their backs turned, didn't I run back, leap over the stile, race through the field and, near a spreading bush, I went to ground!! I lay there, my heart thumping, waiting for the rest of the gang to come back looking for me, baying like hounds.

It didn't happen. Nobody came back. I later learned they didn't miss me until they were inside the school gate and then it was too late. So there I was, lying under a bush at 9.30 in the morning, having passed through stage 1. It was now up to me to make or mar the rest of the day and it took me only one second to decide - on with the fun!

I waited a short while until I felt safe and then I walked back through the field, taking care not to be seen. I came out at Knockaculleen road and had half a mile of open road to travel, so I had to be extra vigilant. Once I had to jump into an old ruin, and tumbled straight into a patch of nettles, when I saw a man cycling round the turn. He passed by whistling and I waited until I calmed down and then up and out - racing for the road like a shot out of a gun. I reached O'Dea's meadow and at last I could rest, but to be extra careful, I made off as far as the boreen where I sat down inside a wall and just listened. And in hindsight, the most abiding memory I have of that day is not the satisfaction of having "codded" my friends, not the delight in having a whole free day to spend as I liked - it was the utter and complete joy of listening to the sounds around me, sounds which I have never forgotten. I heard dogs barking nearby and far away, cows lowing, calves screeching, farmers shouting, carts rumbling, sheep bleating, hens cackling and, above all, birds singing. They sang and twittered. They hopped around. They pecked at flies or berries. They landed for seconds on bushes and stone walls. They were all there - robins, sparrows, wrens, blackbirds, stares, and some inquisitive big black crows who came to view the situation. I stayed motionless, in case I frightened them away.

I thoroughly enjoyed observing them, and I know they enjoyed me because suddenly, feeling hungry, I took out my lunch and shared it with them. I had two slices of brown bread and butter and a jam sandwich, which consisted of two slices of "spotted dick", or raisin bread spread with jam and folded over. I had a bottle of milk as well and did I enjoy my lunch!

I shared the crumbs with my feathered friends and time fled. Looking up at the sun I noticed that it had grown dim. Heavens! It must be running on towards three o'clock and I really should be homeward bound. I "streeled" along the boreen and finally reached our gate.

The minute I put my foot inside the gate, I knew I had made a mistake. My mother was just taking up a cake, one of her early morning chores, and stopped in her tracks when she saw me. So I blurted out to her, "I mitched to-day". "Well", she said, "if you did, you made a bad job of it, because it's only 12 o'clock. However, now that you're here, grab a bite and then run down with the tea to your father in Gort a' Chlobhair opposite the Big House. And you'd better have a good excuse for him - he'll be disappointed in you."

So the first hurdle was safely jumped. I ate and chattered and I ended up by saying "I only did it to see would I succeed," and, in her wisdom, she replied, "Well, I hope you won't try flying to see if you'll succeed."

Taking the lunch bag, I tripped off down the road as far as the windmill over by Droichead Beag and stood looking at my father as he ploughed the garden. Seagulls circled and swooped and the smell of the brown, newly-turned earth was in the air. My father stopped at the headland and hung the oats bag over the horse's neck who immediately started munching and tossing his head. Then he walked to the wall and sat on a grassy mound, all done in silence. He took off his hat, wiped his brow and said, "Well?" I thought, tell the truth and then enjoy the rest of the day, so I told him "I didn't go to school today, I turned back at the Chapel."

I nearly collapsed when, in between "bites and sups", he smiled and said, "I did it myself in my day, so it's nothing new." I sat down beside him and asked him, "Tell me what happened." "My father died when I was 4 years", he said, "and I really hated school. I mitched a few times but didn't really enjoy the aloneness of the day. So I hit on a great idea. I had a marvellous sheep dog, Shep, and he and I got on very well. So one day when I ran off from school, didn't I whistle and call my dog who, lying outside the front door, heard me and headed off towards the small wood like a bullet. We had a great day together and this continued for about a week. But my mother, having noticed the dog's sudden disappearances, followed him and found the two of us - Shep and myself - hunting. She brought me back by the ear and that ended my "outside school adventures".

I was so happy sitting there, listening to my father describing his youthful escapades and adding a little word of caution, "But if I were you," he said, "I wouldn't try it too often, as I mightn't be in such a good mood as I'm in today." I never mitched again - and wouldn't really recommend it, not unless two or three friends do it together!

Totally different from the journey to school was the journey home - long, slow, easygoing, leisurely, no rushing, no worrying, no lone cyclist in the distance. Boys and girls all travelled together - hunting in packs. Whatever one did, all did. We ate things that grew wild - blackberries, nuts, haws, sloes and wild plums in season. Very often we arrived home with purple-stained mouths and fingers from too many blackberries, or tummy aches from too many sloes. We saw hares, rabbits and foxes, studied them silently for a while, and then barked like dogs until the poor animals fled in terror. We picked buttercups, bluebells, cowslips and mayflowers on the roadsides and hedgerows. We climbed walls to look at newly-born, milk-sucking, tail-flicking baby lambs, while their ewe-mothers stamped their feet, telling us to go away and mind our own business. We kept very quiet and still while we gazed at the long-legged, staggering, gawky foals, playing "nose to nose" with their watchful, mare mothers. We fell silent and stood to attention when we spotted a huge, nose-ringed bull, grazing greedily in a field, and we scattered all sides, when he threw up his head and looked at us. We listened attentively for the first call of the cuckoo as we knew of, and believed in the old proverb, "Nuair a labhrann an chuach ar crann gan duilliúr, díol do bhó agus ceannaigh arbhar" - When the cuckoo calls from a leafless tree (very early in the year) sell your cow and buy corn. Indications that a bad harvest will follow a too early advent of the cuckoo. We followed and caught, named, examined and later freed, butterflies - cabbage-white and red admiral, mostly. We sat in meadows and strung daisy-chains, which we hung round our foreheads or necks, and pranced around singing or chanting nursery rhymes. We counted swallows as they swished and knifed in and out through barns, or watched them as they gathered on housetops or walls, preparing for their long, hard, dangerous journey overseas.

Once, I remember, somebody called from the road side, and we all approached, fingers to lips, cautioning silence. A ladybird or God's cow had settled on a girl's hand, and there followed an examination of the little creature, until suddenly she flew away as if to say "What a curious lot".

We lined the banks of the roads, standing in, or kneeling on, green grass, ferns, sometimes neantóga or nettles, looking in admiration at the farmer as he ploughed from headland to headland, with one or two cart horses, while overhead the screeching gulls, wheeled and circled, diving every now and then to pick up a careless worm.

Once a halt was called, when we found an injured pup on the roadside. To leave him there was unthinkable, but how to carry him home? The problem was solved by emptying the books out of the biggest satchel and the pup was lovingly placed in the space and carried home to Fahys, the local public house, where he was immediately recognised and word was sent to his owner. In this way, we learned compassion and caring and toleration.

Often on seeing a lark rising straight up out of a meadow, we waded knee-deep through the long grass, through the feochadáns or thistles, through the dandelions or piss-in-beds, through the red drooping poppies, hoping to find the nest, which we were convinced was there. Maybe it was, but we never found it, and thus we learned how to cope with disappointments.

When hunger attacked us, and it often did, we invaded a garden of ripe turnips, pulled one, whacked it against a rock and ate the pieces which fell off.

With great pleasure, I look back on those happy, happy days, and it seems that freedom was the keynote, and the most enjoyable part of those trips to and from school. There was freedom from the classroom, freedom from the clock and freedom from parental eyes. Indeed, we also enjoyed freedom from restricting boots and shoes - as we kicked them off at the first opportunity, tied their laces together and swung them round our necks, as we raced barefoot and carefree through the countryside.

We went to school in winter weather too, with red noses, wind-blown hair and chilblained hands and feet. We wore high laced boots, thick knitted knee socks, and heavy coats and trudged along in rain or hail. When snow lay on the ground, we indulged in snow-ball throwing which, on a few occasions, "turned dirty", so I usually left them at it and raced away home. We often built a snowman in the school playground, but it melted as soon as the sun appeared. Maybe once every winter, a heavy frost helped us to make a few slides - even though, very often, our backsides kissed the ground and we had nobody to blame only ourselves. Indeed, winter had its compensations because sometimes, if we got terribly wet going to school, the teachers allowed us to stand round the firescreen and "dry off", once the school fire got going. This free time was worth enduring the biting wind and drenching rain.

The sight of the crows, as they wended their way homewards, often alterted us to the fact that time was passing, and chores awaited us at home. So we all separated, called "See ye tomorrow", and ran home as fast as our legs could carry us.

Truthfully, these journeys remain highlights of my youthful schoolgoing days. We chose to tolerate what had to be tolerated - school - so we could enjoy the journey.

Learning was done through discovery and research, rather than by repetition. In later life, I have always felt a sneaking sympathy for children who travel to and from school by bus or car. They are never allowed to discover, what's under **that** stone? what's behind the big rock? what's growing in the field? In my view, they miss out on some unique, wonderful and useful lessons, in which, thank God, we were so fortunate to partake going to and from school.

Our local two teacher National School was first opened on January 1st, 1852. There were fifty pupils attending and each had to pay a penny a week school fees. Down through the years, the building had deteriorated somewhat so, by the time I got there in the mid-thirties, it was really in poor shape.

There were two classrooms and a hall or porch to the front, which was used as a cloakroom. A coalshed was built outside and to the right. Down at the bottom of the playground were the outdoor toilets - one for the boys and one for the girls. The junior classes were taught in the inside room, while the seniors studied in the outside room. When the question, "An bhfuil cead agam dul amach más é do thoil é?" was answered by "Tá", the junior had to walk out through the master's room, out through the porch, or cloakroom, go around the breezy corner, run the entire length of the playground in the hailstones, rain or even snow and then visit the toilets. Indeed, to be honest, the distance of the toilets from the classroom very often deterred me from going when I needed to, especially on a bad day when you wouldn't even put out a cat. I found it was much easier to sit on my heels.

On a breezy day, the windows shook and rattled noisily. The front door didn't close too easily, and didn't open too easily, either. Furniture was scarce and primitive enough compared to the luxury and comfort of today's schools. The desks were the old fashioned ones complete with inkwells which were either overflowing or dry and provided much fun. Fires were lit in grates and fed with coal and slack. Ashes were taken out each morning and, very often, getting a fire going and keeping it alight was very hard work indeed. Large firescreens squatted in front of the fires all day, every day, for safety. Sometimes, if we got wet going to school, we were allowed to stand near the firescreen and dry off - oh! those toasting sessions were wonderful, and much giggling and skitting took place.

Even though the place was a bit delapidated and in bad condition, still our teachers insisted that all the jobs be done every morning, and in the evening after school. We had to dust all the furniture, top-up the inkwells, open the windows, clean the mantlepiece and re-arrange the flowers, tidy the press and generally keep the place spick and span. Floors were swept in the evenings and papers picked up around the playgrounds, and windows were closed. We were always expected to do as much as possible to make our classroom surroundings as pleasant as could be.

It was a cold building and an old building, and not a very comfortable one, but somehow we never seemed to mind. We thought of it as our school and we viewed it as our seat of learning. We had never visited any other school and so were not qualified to make comparisons, but accepted it as it was. It wasn't really the building but the teachers who made the difference. They created an atmosphere there which helped us to listen, to learn, to absorb and to retain. We were like blotting paper, ready to soak up anything and everything. As far as I was concerned, school was a place I wanted to be - and this in itself was a tribute to the teachers. They did everything possible to ensure that each pupil left the school with as much education as was necessary to make an honest living in the world. Maps and charts adorned the walls, and a few books filled the shelves in the press. Children filled the seats and teachers imparted the knowledge, and boy, did they ever!

Duras school was an all Irish school - all subjects taught through the native tongue. Many of the pupils were fluent Irish speakers, including my family. We got the Deontas, or grant, every year, which meant that the whole family must be able to converse as Gaeilge. Each child got about £2.00 per year, and had to promise to speak Irish wherever an opportunity presented itself. I didn't find this very difficult as I just loved Irish. As a matter of interest, I still do.

My sister, Mary, who went to school before I did, told me that Mr. Gardiner, who was then principal of Duras N.S., used to come to our house once a week to play cards with my father - singles 25. She was very young, but she remembers looking through the keyhole of the bedroom door at them, as they sat in front of the fire, hunched up over a small table, as if their very lives depended on the game. Later on, Miss Joyce came to teach in Duras and found her way to our kitchen too. Soon after that, Murty Doyle came as a teacher and he also spent many a night in front of our blazing fire. They got married and moved to Dublin and he became a lecturer in Carysfort Training College. Actually, he taught me when I went there as a student and reminisced once or twice about the good old days in Duras. Miss Farrell replaced Miss Joyce. She was the daughter of the local shopkeepers, Michael and Mary Farrell, and went to school in Ennis where she achieved the distinction of coming first in the country in Leaving Certificate Latin. We all envied her having travelled so far and wondered how she could settle down in the country. When my sister, Mary, went to school, the new principal then was Mr. Pat Wynne who was a full time student of Engineering at UCG. This meant that for 3 years they had a succession of different teachers working as substitutes, while he was in College. He was very musical and on his return at the end of each term, he would tell the stories of the operas he had seen and sing some of the songs. The class could sing The Captain of the Pinafore and Figaro and Good Bye, while the teacher whistled the tune. The standard of education was very high and when Mary was in 6th class, they studied The Merchant of Venice and this was a wonderful help when she had the same play in the Intermediate Certificate in Seamount College.

We were taught Irish, English, Maths, History, Geography, Religion, Ceol, and Needlework. History was taught out of Stair Seanchas na hEireann, and was taught in patches so when all of them were juggled together and set into place, we got a crystal clear picture of what our country and its inhabitants had gone through. When I went to Seamount, I knew more than any other pupil about the Penal Laws, Catholic Emanication and the 1916 Rising. Geography was, for me, a delight. Even as young as I was then I had wanderlust. I traced the Amazon on the large wall map, and crossed the Sahara Desert. I travelled through Europe, skipping from Paris to Berlin to Rome, and then I cruised through the Mediterranean calling briefly to Gibraltar. I meandered through India and then on up to Hong Kong before sailing across to Japan. And finally, I looked up all of the places which my mother had visited and which, by now, were familiar to me. We learned the chief towns of each county by heart, and in Irish. Galway towns were - Gaillimh, Béal Áth na Slua, Tuaim, Baile Loch Riach, agus Gort Inse Guaire. You learned them, and retained them, that's all.

Maths I loved. I used to do twenty or thirty sums every night. Sometimes my archrival in this subject, Jimmy Connors, used to do forty sums - and worse than that, he'd get them all right. There was an answer book and once we copied the answers, but sadly got the page wrong. We were justly punished, "not" said the master "because ye had cheated in a minor thing, but so that ye will never cheat in a major issue."

Religion was a subject which was always treated with great respect, and any other subject might be missed in any day - but never religion. At twelve o'clock on the dot, the Angelus was said and then followed by catechism. We learned the answers all off by heart, repeated the seven deadly sins, trotted out the ten commandments, and could recite eight to ten prayers, both in English and in Irish. And may I add that, in my adult life, I was often glad when, in the middle of a religious argument, I could, and did, rattle off an answer which I had learned out of the Long Catechism many moons ago - and which, incidentally, won the argument for me.

The lady teacher also taught needlework to the girls in the whole school. On Friday evening at 2.00 pm, the girls from the master's room all trooped into the junior room, said a prayer and so began the needlework class. It comprised of knitting and sewing and must have been a real headache. I was never any good at the needle, and always envied my teacher her lovely hands and her beautifully manicured nails. She always tried to see each girl's sample at least once per class, and I usually tried to dodge by letting other girls go ahead of me. However, she had my antics well under cover and would call my name, and up I'd go, grubby, badly sewn piece held out for inspection. She would pull out the large stitches which looked like horses' teeth and in two seconds, she'd have the piece straightened out and looking fairly respectable again. She'd give me back my piece with the order, "Ná bí ag caint, a Bhríd, más é do thoil é", an order which I would dutifully obey for five minutes and then the whispering would start all over again. She taught us how to cast on stitches, knit and cast off. She taught us how to knit a pair of socks and how to sew a handkerchief. She taught patching, darning and hemming - had we listened properly to her, we'd be an asset to any man.

But the legacy which I inherited from my teachers and one which I most fully appreciate, is my love of poetry, and my ability to enjoy it - both English and Irish. They recited with feeling and encouraged us to do the same. They explained run-on lines and blank verse and sonnets. They gave us a few verses to learn and next day, taught us to speak passionately, whisper lingeringly or shout menancingly. To the present day, I can recite poetry which I learned in the junior classroom, many years ago and I, in my turn, tried to pass on that precious gift which my teachers gave to me.

Of course, we got the odd slap, the rap on the knuckles, the tweak of the ear, but we deserved them and there was never any resentment, or anger or displeasure. Our parents agreed that there were school rules as well as home rules and if you disobeyed, well, then suffer the consequences. Just simple philosophy.

Playtime was spent in the playground when you had eaten your lunch. We played jackstones, carrying, blind-man's-buff, tip, colours or hide and seek. Once or twice we got a ball, but it either got lost or did some damage to the windows. On a very wet day, we were allowed to stay in the classroom and read - and we were avid readers. There weren't too many books on the press shelf but what were there, I had read three or four times, Red Cloud, Blackcock's Feather, The Heroes of the Dawn, Robinson Crusoe, and Helen of Troy. I have never enjoyed books as much as I enjoyed those, and re-reading them only added to the enjoyment.

The tempo of the classroom, which usually was calm and serene, was sometimes rocked by the advent of the cigire. This happened maybe once a year. Indeed, he need never have visited us, as the work went along solidly, day after day, week after week, year after year, whether anybody was looking over our shoulders or not. However, he did come and, instinctively, we knew it, when a long brown envelope landed on the master's desk and, on being opened, held a single sheet of paper with two or three lines of writing in the middle. A look of apprehension usually crossed his face and then he sent the letter in to Miss Farrell. That evening, he'd tell us to revise the history dates, hot up on the tables and learn at least one poem each. He also threatened us not to miss a day for the next week or so. We knew then that the cigire's visit was indeed imminent, and that the master was trying to make sure that we wouldn't disgrace him. For myself, I couldn't care less about an inspector, but for others it was like a sword hanging over their heads. One boy called Willie, who didn't really shine in the classroom, said to me once, "What does the inspector ask me questions for? - sure I couldn't tell him anything that he doesn't know already."

Having received the letter telling of the coming visit, the master used to walk a lot - up and down, back and forth, in and out - around the room - a short nervous walk, while he pondered whether he should lead us or drive us to do our best. Any thoughts of mischief which we might have been contemplating, vanished as we somehow recognised the unspoken cry for help. After all, he was our master, it was our school and we weren't going to let him down. So we set to it with a will and learned more in that week than in any ordinary month - spellings, tables, history, geography, Irish, English, were all taken out and dusted. On the specified morning, the master would come in early and re-distribute the brainboxes around the room. He'd dot those whom he termed above average here and there through the classroom, like raisins in a soda cake, or railway stations around the country. "Sit here you, Jimmy Connors, and you, Miko Fahy, and answer out the history". They were infallible at history, and battles and dates. "Come over here, Bridie Quinn and Julia, and put up your hands for the Irish questions". We were fairly good at the cúpla focal, especially the briathra neamh-rialta – which the inspector loved, may God forgive him. To Kitty Hynes and Bernie Mahon, he'd say "Clear your throats and sing out loud and clear". They were both lovely singers and could do "Adown by the Glenside" better than anybody else. "Máire and Paddy, sit in between those boys and girls and shout out the spellings". Mary Carty and Paddy Linnane were dingers at the spellings and the meanings. And, finally, he'd tell Delia Hynes and Mattie Glynn, "Trot out the tables, the pair of you, and sit one at each end of that desk". They were simply super at tables and never called a wrong answer. An so the master, like a war general, prepared the battlefield in a devious, yet simple, way. "Rita", he'd finally say to Rita Keane, "You'll open and close the door when he comes in". Rita was very pretty and sat near the door, ready to admit the visitor. He also prayed that the funny man of the classroom would be quiet and said out of the corner of his mouth, "Agus dún do bhéal tusa". "What did he say?" your man would ask and we'd be blunt and tell him, "Shut up, you".

Suddenly, the inspector appeared at the door, silent and cat-footed. Rita let him in and we all stood to attention. There he was, a giant in a brown suit with kind of patches on his elbows, a small black book in his hand. "Lean ar aghaidh", was his usual admonition, and so class continued. Soon we forgot he was there and when the command, "Lámha suas" came, up shot our hands, fingers clicking and a broad smile would transfix the master's face as if to say to the inspector, "Look at that will you? Aren't they great?". Then he would take over the class himself and no matter what questions he asked, hands would be raised all over the room, as we were so strategically placed.

Once there was a funny incident which, to this day, brings a smile to my face. On this particular day, the inspector examined the roll-book and found a name with a great number of absent marks after it. He called out "Seas suas, Seán O Loinsigh". After much prodding and elbowing from us, we got Seán to his feet, a worried look on his moon face.

"Well, Séan", said the inspector. "I see that you spend a lot of time away from school".

Séan said, "Yes, sir."

Inspector, "Now tell me what did you do when you were at home yesterday?"

Séan, "Helpin' at the threshin, sir."

Inspector, "And had ye a big crowd?"

Séan, "Oh yes, sir, we had a great meitheal".

Inspector, "Good boy. Now let's see how many of the meitheal can you name?"

Séan then took a deep breath and listed out the neighbours' nicknames - "The Gasses, Cork, The Geatar, Gug, Gloineach, Tom Mhairtín, The Síóg, Tommy Mhicil, Bodhrán, Sonny Mhairtín, Jack and," he finished triumphantly, "The Pope".

The inspector was highly amused and after a few seconds, said, "Now then, and how was the Pope?" Sean by this time was thoroughly enjoying himself,and, thinking he was doing the master a great favour, he leaned across the seat confidentially and said, "My mother said that the Pope was a bloody hoor – he ate twice as much as everybody else".

Of course, the entire class was convulsed with laughter, and it took a couple of wallops of the stick on the blackboard to bring us back to normality. The inspector smiled happily, and Sean sweated profusely and I'm sure the master vowed to decapitate each and every one of us later at his leisure. However, things worked out well and soon we were let out to play, while the two men settled down to eat the sandwiches prepared by Mrs Moylan, while the master explained the nicknames to our distinguished visitor.

Many teachers taught in Durus N.S., for example: Miss Joyce, Mr. Doyle, Mr. Markham, Mr. O'Friel, Mr. Vaughan, Mr. McHugh and Mr. Wynne - all impressive and wonderful people. But those whom I remember best, and those to whom I have always been grateful were Miss Kathleen Farrell and Mr. Kieran Moylan. Born in Peterswell, near Gort, Kieran was - and still is - a fine singer and musician who often featured on radio and television. The lady taught the juniors and the gentleman taught the seniors. They were dedicated, hardworking, fair and interested. They recognised our potential, and urged us to try to do well. They set before us a very high standard of ideals and, for the majority of us, I must say we have tried to live up to them ever since.

I personally thank them both for teaching me so well, and for fostering in me a love of learning - an urge to accept a challenge and a will to achieve.

Gura maith agaibh, a mhuinteoirí ionmhana.
Go mbeirimid beo ag an am seo arís.

Haymaking

When I was young, the summers seemed longer and hotter than they are now. The bees droned more busily and the cabbagewhite butterflies flitted more tantalisingly. The cuckoo's call sounded more clearly across the meadows, and the children shrieked more playfully. Looking back, I honestly think that all things looked and sounded better and happier than they do now.

Every summer - early summer - haymaking was an important part of life on the farm. At that time, hay was cut or mown by scythe - swath after swath. One minute the grasses were standing up, waving in the breeze, cheerfully inviting birds and insects to come and nestle in the cosy scented warmth. Next minute, the grasses lay "dead" on the ground, inert, unable to wave, murdered by the scythe. Holding it by two 'doirníns' or handles, my father wielded the scythe skilfully across the ripe meadow of hay, as he carefully cut a swath the width of the scythe. This definitely required skill and manipulation as I soon found out when, while my father's back was turned, I tried it and almost cut the legs off myself.

Our main meadow was down by Bóithrín hAinlí past Tobar Pháraic. It was a big field with awkward corners, so my father usually got two local young men, Mattie Quinn and Mickey Keane, to help him to mow the hay. They were great "yarners" or could put a great skin on a yarn, and when my father would see them - standing up, scythe handle resting on the ground, sharpening stone in hand - telling us yarns, he'd yell, "Dammit, why don't ye do a bit of work, or 'twill soon be night."

Nowadays, when I get the never-to-be forgotten smell

of newly mown hay, I am immediately transported to that main meadow of long ago. It ran parallel to three other neighbours' fields, so it was that we often found ourselves turning, tossing, raking, cocking or tramming hay, while the neighbours and their children did the same next door. We called across to each other in a happy and lighthearted way; we flirted brazenly and blushingly - with two fields between us and the whole village looking on, and we cemented friendships which lasted all our lives. The Linnanes, Glynns, Hynes's, Fahys and Kavanaghs all went through the purgatory of haymaking, just like we did.

Towards evening, should we in our meadow have the hay cocked first and were told to go home, we all jumped the neighbours' walls and helped them to finish up. If, on the other hand, we had been "laxtering" and loitering during the day, as was often the case, and our neighbours were ready to go, but we were not, they all swarmed into our meadow and amid much laughter, shouting, yelling and repartee, helped with the job in hand. My goodness! but my father hated this invasion. He hated to see them coming and, indeed, didn't hesitate to tell them - "Belt off home", he would say, "I declare to God ye do more harm than good. Ye're like bees swarming all over the meadow, but not half as useful." Of course, they all laughed and under their breath said, "If we're the bees, then your daughters must be the honey." That great sense of friendship was there among the neighbours, you could say anything you liked and nobody got angry or annoyed.

The threat of rain, and therefore ruination of the crop of hay, was always used by grown-ups to keep us working and on our toes. "See those woolpack clouds up there, if we don't hurry, they'll burst and the hay will be ruined." We always looked, but never saw any threatening woolpacks. Nevertheless, we humoured them and kept them happy and tossed and turned with a will. Raking was a job I hated above every other evil, and it was one I always seemed to be left with.

"Get that rake, Bridie, and rake out from the wall".

"Which wall?"

"That wall", and that wall looked to me at the time like the Great Wall of China. It went on and on and on. No sooner had I raked a few yards, when along came a playful gust of wind and blew all the hay right back to the wall again. At that precise moment, my father would look over and say, "Do you know what, if you don't start soon, 'twill be night on you". To which I'd usually reply, "But I had it raked and the wind blew it back again". Quick as a flash he'd reply, "Don't be danach (or daft). Sure there's no wind". And back I had to go and rake "out from the wall" all over again. Left to myself I wouldn't have raked at all, but to my father not to rake was one of the seven deadly sins. So we raked, behind every rock, around every bush and in every nook and corner - not on one day but every day, because raking was on the daily agenda.

We usually arrived in the meadow around ten o'clock, when all the dew had disappeared. After a short time of spasmodic laughing and talking, we would all settle down and work would be going along nicely, when suddenly, with a wild shriek, one of us would throw down a fork or rake, and run pell-mell through the meadow with a swarm of angry bees in hot pursuit. My father would pull off his hat and slap away the buzzing bees from the victim's head and hair. Then he would go slowly and cautiously in search of the honey in the hive. When he located the site, he would go down on one knee while we all stood around, peering excitedly, glad of any distraction from the work. He would brush aside the hay and reveal dozens of tiny honey-combs nestling in a mossy hole in the ground. He never seemed to mind the bees which buzzed frantically around him. Neither did he believe in rooting out the whole hive - no, he just took out enough to give everybody a taste. He would lift up a honey comb and sqeeze it, and golden sticky honey dripped from it. Eager hands were outstretched for a helping, carefully licked with one hand held underneath, in case one precious drop got lost. Oh! How deliciously sweet, how deliciously sticky.

After this delightful sticky interval, work would start again amid an excited babble of voices, and a lot of lip-licking and mouth smacking. Tummy rumblings would tell us that soon it would be lunch time, so many hopeful glances were cast up towards the back of our house, easily seen from the meadow, to see if there were any movements heralding food. In no time at all, another shriek would announce that somebody had spotted my mother coming down through the sheeps' field with the tea. As she reached the road, she left one basket outside the wall and one inside. Then she stepped out over the stile, and lifted the inside basket out. Now, taking the two baskets, she headed off again for the meadow. By this time, we could contain ourselves no longer. We would throw down our "weapons", jump the cocks, knocking some and, in spite of calls from my father, we raced to meet her. We helped her with the two baskets filled with goodies.

My father, having failed to stop our exodus from the meadow, would think to himself - "If you can't lick them, join them". He would pick a sheltered spot, away from the wind, where we would all congregate. My mother would spread a large white cloth on the ground and then unfold the feast - fruity scones or buns, dripping with butter, sometimes still hot; spotted dick or currant cake and slices of brown bread, liberally spread with newly-churned butter and covered again with jam. Last of all, she would carefully lift out the huge apple cake - golden brown and sugary. No talk about calories or cholesterol then! There was a huge enamel pot of tea, kept warm surrounded by papers and dressed in a homemade knotted cap. A jar full of sugar and a big bottle of milk completed the feast. My father was served first and then our rumbling tummies were satisfied. No food has ever tasted as good as the food in the meadow, no tea as sweet. When my own children were growing up and we didn't have a farm, I "hired" them out to a local farmer and his family, for a long summer's day or two haymaking, so that they could sample the unequalled glory of tea and food in the meadow.

While we ate, we talked and laughed. Sometimes, those in the next meadow shouted and whistled, as their food might not have arrived yet. Having stuffed ourselves, we lay back, full, well-fed and happy, and if the dreaded threatening woolpack clouds had swung right above us just then and burst into rain, we couldn't have cared less.

Occasionally, if something unusual had happened in the far away capital of Dublin, which to us was off in another world, my mother brought the newspaper and his glasses to my father. Having smoked a pipe full of tobacco, he would put on his glasses and read the main headlines. He would leave the small print to be read in the evening in a more comfortable and leisurely fashion. So lunch time passed and "all was right with our world".

After a short time, my father would give us good example by standing up and getting back to work, and soon we would all be "up and at it". Once more could be heard the good humoured banter, the happy, highpitched laughter or even the verse of a song, as hay was tossed and turned and cocked, and the sun crept slowly along the blue, blue sky.

When the day's work was over, and the haymaking for that day was ended, we headed home, happy to be free. The meadows looked lonely and silent, hay all cocked and raked, but with nobody there. Sometimes we went to Trácht for a swim, but not often, because we had all the evening chores to do. If we were late coming back, my father would stand at the haggard gate and whistle for us. Pandemonium!

Haymaking days resurrect priceless golden memories, vivid and clear and jealously guarded. How closely we all worked together. How very much we enjoyed the good things of nature - sights and sounds and, of course, smells. To me the smell of new mown hay evokes old fashioned and pleasurable memories.

Et with bad luck

While I was growing up, life was, on the surface, easy-going and friendly. We were "led and said by religion". But, under the surface, we were faced with superstitions and pisreóga. I am not saying that we believed them all. But superstitions were attached to many happenings and when this was so - beware!

Bad sickness, bad luck, infertile wives, low milk yield, bad crops, were supposedly all the results of pisreóga and caused many a headache. Pisreóga were beliefs in certain omens or magical signs. These beliefs were tinged with fear - fear of the mysterious or the unknown. They could be supernatural or religious, or just man-made. These beliefs or opinions or practices were based on folklore or on rumour or, sometimes, on excessive fear of the consequences if the sign or the omen was disobeyed. These consequences would usually be bad luck, ill health, loss of possessions, usually an unhappy kind of retribution. To many superstitions certain rhymes or "charm-words" were attached, and sometimes, no matter how strong minded or positive you were, they would put the fear of God in you. Behind closed doors they were thought up and put into action. Behind closed doors people suffered silently and accepted passively the sometimes imagined results.

In our house spiders were treated with the greatest respect and were never killed - accidently perhaps, but never intentionally. The story was that if you killed a spider of your own free will, you'd be "et" with bad luck. As often happened, when a spider came "in out of the cold" and spun a web in the corner of the kitchen or across the window, somebody just lifted off a thread of the web, with the spider still entangled, and hung it up outside on the gate or on a bush. In this way, the spider spun a new web, and everybody breathed easily again. The explanation of respect for the spider goes back to the days of The Flight into Egypt. When the Holy Family fled from Herod, so the story went, they were pursued by soldiers and hid in a cave. The soldiers were searching all the caves, one by one, and the trio were sitting terrified in one of them waiting to be caught. Suddenly the spiders went into action. They spun their cobwebs across the cave entrance, and when the soldiers came to it, the leader said, "Let's pass this one by. See, nobody has been through its entrance for years. It's choked with cobwebs", and away they went. Thus, the spiders saved the Holy Family and, for this reason, we were taught to save the spiders.

Shattering a mirror into smithereens was just about the worst thing that could happen to anybody. If you broke a mirror, you suffered seven years bad luck. Believe it or not, it's something that, to the present day, brings a shiver of apprehension to me. Of course, it means nothing, but old habits die hard, and what you grow up believing is not easily blown away.

When I was young, a next door neighbour's daughter broke a mirror by accident in a neighbour's house. She ran off home without admitting the breakage to the woman of the house. Next day, she fell off her bicycle. Two days later she hit her thumb with a hammer. One week later, she sprained her ankle. Crying, she told me what had happened and said, "God help me, if this is the way it's going to be for the next seven years". So we chatted it out and she decided to tell the woman of the house about the incident. Off we went together and recounted our story to Molly Sullivan, who laughed so much that she cried a little. "Musha, God help you, a stóirín", she said, "sure that mirror has been broken since the year of dot, long before I came to this house, and what's another crack or two from you". Miraculously, the mishaps and unexplained accidents stopped and my friend had no more bad luck. Could the bad luck events have happened, because they were expected to happen? Could the idea, firmly planted in the mind, have suddenly sprouted and

67

yielded fruit?

In every house, on St. Martin's Eve, a "coileach" was killed and the blood was sprayed outside or over the door to keep away all evil, and keep goodness and good health in the house. This superstition's origin stemmed from the exodus of the Israelites from Egypt. Moses asked the Pharaoh to allow his people to leave, but he refused. God told Moses to tell each Israelite family to kill a lamb, sprinkle the blood over the door and cook and eat the flesh. They did so. That night, an angel of the Lord came, passed over the doors sprayed with blood and killed the first-born in the other homes. And so the superstition was born and, as far as I can gather, is still very much alive, the coileach's blood exhorting evil and bad luck to "Move on! We have a "bloody" good insurance in this house".

Without doubt, meeting a red-haired woman first thing on May morning was bad enough, but meeting one on the way to the fair was disastrous. One of my earliest memories is of my father going to the fair with his neighbour, Thomas Mooney. This happened before we were old enough to go with him, so he had to go with somebody else. Early in the evening, they put the cattle into the field beside the house, so they could be got at easily. They went to bed early, preparing for their midnight start. They left at about 2 am on a cold dreary March morning, so cold my father said later that "'twould freeze the nose off a brass monkey".

They had to drive the cattle to the fair in Kinvara to be in time to catch the early jobbers. Snug in my warm bed, I remember listening to the noises from the kitchen as my father and Thomas ate breakfast, murmuring low in case they woke up the lot of us at that hour; then the scraping of chairs, the creaking of the door, the belting of their hobnailed boots on the front street and the calls of the cattle. A few shouts, the dog barking and then all the noises receded as they walked away up the road.

At this point sleep took over as, in my drowsy imagination, I walked with them up the road, past the Mount where the cattle would surely try to make a dash for it, through Nogra, when again the cattle would endeavour to escape and on up the road to Geata Bán. On reaching this gateway, they would meet many other farmers and all together would converge on Kinvara. I slept.

Then suddenly, they were back again, and this early return was not good news at all and I was apprehensive. However, things settled down and it was not until next day that I heard what had happened. "No sooner had we gone out on the high road at Geata Bán," said my father, "than we saw this woman driving an ass and cart. That wasn't bad enough, but I declare to God, wasn't she a red-haired woman as well - Cáit Rua from Currenrue. That was the last straw and it was just as well for us to turn back as we knew she'd put "the bad eye" on the cattle, and we'd have to sell them for half price". So this irrational belief - that if you meet a red-haired woman first thing on your way to the fair - meant that two sensible men were so credulous that they actually turned back for fear of the bad eye of the "Cailín rua".

Churning was done in most homes in the kitchen, using a dash-churn. The cream was put into the churn, and the "dash" was whacked up and down, and this pounding went on until butter formed. If a neighbour called for any reason, either to "rest his bones" or to chat, he would immediately be expected to put his hand to the dash. If he didn't, then the bean an tí knew that there would be no butter in the churn as it would have followed the visitor. By not putting his hand to the dash and by wishful thinking, he would have "spirited" away the butter. Maggie Hynes often said that the best thing was to do the churning out the back where no visitors could come. I think she was right, but somehow the kitchen was the usual place and, if a visitor stepped over the threshold with a hearty "God bless all here", put a hand to churn dash, pounded it up and down a few times, then all was well and there would be "im go leor" when the churning was over.

There is a species of the crow family called the magpie. He is black with white underpants, and more than half of his 18 inch length is a wedge-shaped tail. He is a thieving bird, and chatters a lot as he hops around. One, five or eight magpies bring bad luck and sorrow. There was a rhyme attached to the number of them we saw:

"One for bad luck
Two for good luck
Three for joy
Four to get married
Five to die
Six for silver
Seven for gold
Eight for Heaven as we are told".

Occasionally, we changed things to suit ourselves. If we saw only one magpie, we said "one for good luck", then went happily on our way, secure in the knowledge that somehow we had, for the moment anyhow, pushed aside bad luck.

Buried eggs in a field could result in failed crops. Or should I say, eggs were buried in the hope that failed crops would result. Some farmers buried the eggs always before May 1st, usually a clutch of glugars or bad eggs, in a field of another farmer, in the hope that all bad luck, either in health or crops or animals would go with them. The eggs would be discovered when the farmer was ploughing the land in the spring time or saving the hay. Sometimes on discovery, the farmer just threw the eggs in the bushes. Sometimes he burned them and sometimes he threw holy water over them to break the alleged spell. Of course, sometimes nothing bad ever happened, but that didn't mean that there wasn't a belief in the pisreóg, and a farmer could be very upset and anxious after finding a "clutch of bogáns or glugars" in the headland. Although, how buried eggs could ruin crops or bring bad luck was always beyond my understanding.

There was a rhyme which said "A whistling woman and crowing hen, always comes to some bad end". Well, my youngest sister, Julia, and I were avid whistlers and when people, especially older ones, heard us, they shook their heads, looked pityingly at us as if to say "Your doom is sealed, you'll never come to anything good". However, I'm glad to say that we never suffered any misfortune or ill-luck as a result of our whistling and now we view it as a load of rubbish.

So it was that pisreóga had a superficial effect on our lives and even the clergy had no wish to overrule the superstitious beliefs. Changing house, starting a building or beginning anything new, was always done on a Friday - just as is done in the present day. But when the Friday also happened to be the 13th of the month, then there was a distinct problem. I remember an incident told by my father when Ellen Duane was about to move into her new little house and the chosen Friday was the 13th, something Ellen didn't realise until Monday of the week. She worried about moving on Friday 13th and got different pieces of advice from different people, but wasn't happy. So off she went to the local priest, and asked him what she should do. His answer was "Ná bris reacht is ná déan reacht" - don't break a rule and don't make a rule. So he advised her to "make the change on the following Friday, the 20th. "And don't tell anybody that I said so", he said, "because what they don't know won't worry them. But don't think I believe in that rigmarole, 'cos I don't." I think he did!

These were but a few of the beliefs that pervaded the society in which I grew up and which definitely coloured the way our parents thought. Some of the superstitions had, to our knowledge, no known origin, but grew from the ramblings of an old man, or the mumblings of an old woman. Never open an umbrella in the house. Bad luck follows if a robin flies in the window. If you spill salt, a row is on the horizon. Hear an ass braying, you will hear of a sudden death. The list was endless and, passively, we went along with belief in superstitions. When one of us decided to jump the traces, and do exactly what the pisreóg told us not to do, then the grown-ups blessed themselves and muttered, "God help you, you'll end up badly, if you aren't gone before that". But we didn't and supersition still prevails. For any money, I wouldn't walk under a ladder or, when I spill salt, I get ready for the row which is supposed to ensue. Am I et with bad luck!?

Tom and Seán

Tom and Seán Mhairtin Fahy were two brothers who lived in Parkmore in a small thatched house, whitewashed outside and beautifully clean inside. A gate and a stile led into it. We always ignored the gate and, jumping the stile, swung on the half door which was latched on the inside. We could then look straight across at the opposite kitchen wall on which hung a weights clock. Never since have I seen one like it, or half as fine. It was a great beauty and had been bought at an auction in "The Big House" down the road.

When he was young, Tom Fahy walked to the docks in Galway with John Quinn, my uncle. They boarded a liner bound for America and off they went - just like that. It was said that Tom's brother, Seán, spent most of the time while Tom was gone standing on the wall outside his house, looking up the road to see if he could see "sight or light" of him. He confided to his neighbour, Denny Hynes, "'Pon my soul, I don't know where he's gone, if the ground didn't open and swallow him".

The voyage across the Atlantic took many weeks and, in later years, Tom said they had two very bad storms. He said that one of the crew was swept overboard but nobody even threw him a rope as it was every man for himself. Tom and John had only two or three shillings each when they joined the ship so, during the voyage, they had to earn at least pocket money. Tom taught the Belgian Captain some Irish phrases in return for "a few bob" - ones like

"Dún do bhéal"
"Póg mo thóin"
"Tóram Póg".

What they meant didn't make any difference to the captain, said Tom, and every evening he hummed a tune, putting the Irish words to the music. An old Irish sailor taught Tom how to carve wooden objects and those he sold to the more wealthy passengers. This particular craft helped him when he returned from his travels and he carved some lovely things for friends. John Quinn also had to earn his fare and did so by helping the purser or "money man", as he was very quick and sure at figures and money. At least they proved very resourceful and showed that they would never die of hunger.

Finally, they arrived in New York where Tom only stayed two days, until he boarded another liner, bound for Cobh. He recounted many funny stories about his travels. Funnily enough, he'd never ask to go back. "Once was enough to last me a lifetime", he used to say. He loved to chat with my mother about America because she herself had spent some years in it.

He had a calm crossing, during which Tom said "I saw a man pointing a loaded gun at another man". I asked, "did he kill him?" "How would I know?", said Tom, "Sin é, that's it, I didn't wait to see".

Anyhow, he walked home from Cobh and finally reached Parkmore. He came through the half door just as Seán was dishing up pig's head and cabbage. Seán said afterwards, "I nearly collapsed in my standing when I saw him". Tom loved to start with "Glory be to God, I never saw the like...". Years later, when somebody asked him why did he go to America at all, Tom always answered, "I only went over to see the time...". By golly, it was a dear time check, albeit an interesting one. By the way, John Quinn never came back to Duras; he got married, reared a family and never saw his native village again.

Neither Tom nor Seán could read or write. Once a leter came and Tom was sick and so it fell to Seán to take it to somebody to read it. He left it on the kitchen table for half a day, staring at it as if it would bite. He circled it, felt it, stared at it and finally took it up to my father to read. When he heard the address - "Local Government Board" - he interrupted and asked "Meas tú, Michael, cén sórt fear é the Local Government Board?" My father said, "It's not one man at all. It's about 10 men". Poor Seán! He almost fainted and said in a crying voice, "Ó go bhfóire Dia orm. It's ten of them against one of me". At this point, my father had read the letter and could satisfy Seán that it wasn't a bad letter at all and there was no need to worry.

Tom, as I have already said, loved to carve things out of wood and made chairs, and camáns. He also put up a half-loft in our kitchen, from the fireplace to the front door, across the ceiling and it was of great value. It was used as a safe place for storing precious things and our Sunday shoes were polished early in the week and left along the edge of the loft. As well as buying his lovely clock at an auction in the Big House he also bought an old broken piano. Believe it or not, he carved the most beautiful cradle from it and presented it to my mother when her first baby was born. It cradled all four girls in my family and was then passed on to another family of six children, who were all reared in "perfect harmony" without a flat or sharp note!! Just imagine being rocked to sleep next to middle C!

After coming back from New York, Tom was a local celebrity. People asked him all kinds of questions and, to be honest, he gave them all kinds of answers. He liked to tell one particular story about New York. He said that when he arrived in the city, "I went walking down the street looking up at the high buildings with my mouth open". He couldn't get over all the lovely big shops, when suddenly an American appeared at the window of a second storey house and called down to Tom,

"Hello, Paddy, what are you gaping at?"

Tom answered, "I'm looking at the fine big houses".

The Yank said, "Oh! You'll have to move on up the street before you see the really big ones. Feast your eyes on them, Paddy, sure these are only stables compared to them".

And Tom answered, "I was thinking well that these were only stables when I saw you looking out the stable window, like an ass".

Of course, we never had any proof that it had happened at all, but Tom loved to use his imagination.

Now and then, Tom got some repair work to do at the Big House. Sometimes, he stayed overnight as the house was always empty. But Tom firmly and repeatedly said that every night at the stroke of midnight, an old man's figure shuffled out of a room, down the hall to a press full of papers, where he searched and searched for half an hour, before shuffling back to the room where he began his journey. Obviously he never found anything because he never carried anything back with him. When I asked him about whom he thought it was, he always said, "Sure, it was Count de Basterot doing his hell".

"Why didn't you ask him what he was looking for?" I said.

And his very logical answer was, "Sin é, that's it, if he wanted to tell me, didn't he know well I was there!!" And I admit I couldn't argue with that.

Once I visited while Tom was baking a cake. When well kneaded, he put it on the skillet on the red hot coals, and in no time at all it was baked on one side and ready to be turned. He tossed it over, and very handy he was too, and baked the other side. When it was ready, the lovely "fresh bread" smell filled the small kitchen. Tom left the cake out on the window sill to cool, sat on the stone seat outside to smoke a "gail" while keeping an eye on the cat who also fancied the cake, "Cogar mé seo leat", said Tom, "If I don't watch him, he'll have it between his whiskers in no time at all." So Tom sat and smoked, while the cat watched and waited and the cake cooled and Seán stepped up to the half-door now and again, looking from screwed-up eyes in his wizened little face and all was right with their world.

On another visit, I watched him making soup. He boiled a chicken or maybe it was a hen - scrawny and scraggy-looking enough, I must say. He threw in two big onions, peeled but uncut. He chopped in a carrot and parsnip, which he had grown in his cabbage garden, and he boiled the lot. When I looked into the small black pot as it hung from the hanger, it was bubbling away doing nicely, with "súilíní" or "globules of fat" bobbing, bubbling and dancing along on top. "Sin é, that's it", said ever generous Tom. "Drink a sup, 'twill put hair on your chest." As that was precisely the last thing I wanted, I graciously declined!

In their very late years, Tom and Seán Fahy decided to have Mass in their home. In other words, they agreed to have the "stations". The neighbours and local girls came in and tidied up the kitchen. Notice I didn't say "cleaned up", because the place was always spotless. Station day dawned. Tom and Seán were up since daybreak and had shaved and put on their grandfather shirts with waistcoats. Tom kept admonishing Seán, "Ná bí ag féachaint le do bhéal" - "Don't be looking with your mouth". A little later he said "Suí síos agus ná bí i do sheasamh cosúil le standpike" - "Sit down and don't be standing up like a standpike".

Up on the dresser, the rashers and sausages were all waiting, as were brown bread and a loaf or two. Seán, all the previous week, had stubbornly insisted that he was certain the "poor sagairtín" would just love cold pig's head and "enough of it". But the local helpers otherwise decided, and now, luckily for the priest, there was a fairly ordinary menu.

The priest arrived and was met outside the door with a lighted candle out of respect. The altar was set up on a table, in front of the dresser. A huge fire blazed on the hearth and the kettle was singing merrily. Soon Mass began, and everything was going nicely.

Just at Offertory time, didn't the cat jump up on the half door, wondering no doubt where was his 10 o'clock saucer of milk. Tom shouted threateningly, "Scut, a dheabhail", and scratched and scraped his boots on the hearth-stones near where he sat. The cat refused to budge. Then Tom threw his cap, the aim was good and the cat went flying out into the street followed by the cap. The priest continued. All was quiet on the kitchen front, but only for 5 minutes. Up leaped the cat again and balanced on the top of the half door with a loud screech, his claws scratching and scraping. Tom let off a racht of a curse, caught a caorán of turf, threw it unerringly, hitting the cat, and knocking it sideways into the middle of the kitchen.

By now the priest had suspended all activities, standing motionless. All of the locals waited motionless as well, trying their best not to make eye-contact with anybody else. Tom heaved himself up and tried to catch the cat, who clawed and spat, and raced from the bedroom door to the dresser and back to the kitchen door. Then Seán went to his aid and between them, they "flocked" the cat and heaved him out over the half door. Everybody then smiled in relief, and Mass continued and all returned to normal.

During the breakfast, Tom turned to the priest and said he was sorry about the cat. The priest was silent for a minute and said, "Why? Sure the poor cat did nothing wrong. He only wanted to be "in on the Mass" as well as you". Tom was struck dumb, and said nothing until the priest had left. Then his comment was "Sin é, that's it, the poor priesteen must be three sheets in the wind! Sure I never heard of a cat going to Mass!"

The two brothers lived a very simple, uncomplicated sort of life, one brother a little more domineering than the other, but nevertheless, living in close harmony for many years. I talked often with them and got two very different views of life and the hereafter. I think that Seán was fully convinced that Tom would "run things on the other side". And Tom thought that in the next world, your hell is undoing or trying to undo all the wrongs you did in this world. And you know, he could be right.

They are buried in Parkmore graveyard. If anybody reading this knew them, or knew of them, kindly pray for them and, who knows, but when our turn comes, they may be able to help us on the "rocky road to Heaven".

Hookers and Púcáns

Nowadays, Cruinniú na mBád is held in Kinvara every year in the month of August, to commemorate the turf trade that once was carried on between Connemara and Duras and Kinvara.

One of my earliest memories is coming out from school, and looking across the bay at the Hookers - maybe five of them - spread across the blue sea, black or brown calico sails flapping in the nifty breeze. They looked exactly like five great sea birds, moving silently and swiftly. They were always low in the water, ploughing along, weighed down with loads of turf taken on board the evening before in Rossaveel or Carraroe. At the quay, the hookers and their boatmen, called Bádóirí, had to sit and wait for the tide to lift off the boat and carry it out to sea and across the bay to Duras or Kinvara. They always hoped to reach Parkmore pier just before high tide.

Boats were manned by strong, hard-working bádóirí – Jimín na nOileán, Na Báileachaigh, Na Griallaisí, Antoine an Bhádóra, and Paitín MacDonncha - to name but a few. They always wore warm clothes needed for the bad weather, sudden squalls and whirlwinds which they met on the crossing. They wore báiníns or white flannel jackets, ceann asna or frieze trousers and head hugging hats, very often tied securely with pieces of rope. Inside the báinín was a home hand knitted jumper, warm and cosy for the sea voyage.

Loads of turf and some provisions were taken on board in Connemara. Sometimes the provisions included a few bottles of poitín. My father often said that when a badóir was cold and damp, and getting colder and damper, if he took a swig of poitín, it would "light a fire in his chest."

When very young, I always felt very sorry for the poor bádoír, in case he'd be burned alive. I needn't have worried - it was a fire which they thoroughly enjoyed, and never feared. To buy a bottle of poitín at that time cost three old shillings and was considered a great luxury indeed.

A hooker had three sails – jib, foresail and mainsail – and moved with stately dignified grace across the choppy or calm waters. Sometimes, if there was a gusty or forceful wind, the boat would "tack" – it sailed from side to side, from left to right, from right to left, in a zig zag manner, in order to diffuse and break up the force of the wind. This tacking needed great dexterity and immense strength as well as expert local sea knowledge to manoeuvre the boat through the dangerous channels and hidden under currents. The bádóirí had all of these qualities and were in truth masters of the sea.

Sometimes, the turf was brought from Connemara to the pier in Parkmore in a púcán or a gleoiteog - much smaller and lighter boats than the hookers. These smaller boats naturally carried smaller loads of turf and moved very swiftly. A hooker load of turf cost £5 and a púcán load of turf cost £3. Each boat had certain identification marks either in the colour or shape of their main sails. My father used to stand at our haggard gate and look across the bay at the boats as they sailed close to the wind and he could identify each and every one of them correctly.

When the boats docked at the pier, the bádóirí usually visited the local public house, Fahys, for two reasons - to drink a well earned pint and to meet up with buyers for their turf loads. This sale of turf was easy enough, as there were no bogs in our area and each household needed at least one load of turf per year. At times, when money was scarce, two farmers went "in co" and split one load between the two of them. Sometimes, if a farmer needed turf very badly, he gave a bádóir some éarlais or éarnais - deposit money in good faith that the next load would be brought quickly and would be good. At that time, they all depended on the boats as the roads were not good enough to transport the turf - that came much later. On arrival, whether at the pier or in the public house, a certain length of time was spent making a bargain and slapping palms, and hand spitting and finally, hand shaking. Then the bádóirí returned to their boats, and unloaded the turf on to the pier - sod by sod, sod by sod. This was not a nice job, especially on a windy day, because of flying turf dust. Soon horses and carts came, were filled up and then made their way home to the haggard where the reek of turf was built. The neighbours usually helped and before the farmer knew where he was, the turf was home, safe and sound, thanks to the "meitheal". Later on, the reek was thatched to keep it dry and snug. Down on the pier, a job of work still had to be done - all the tiny pieces of turf called "caoráns" had to be picked into bags out of the turf dust and turf mould. These "caoráns" were really cherished by the bean an tí, and were kept to rekindle the fire in the early morning. Even the turf mould was used - it was brought home and thrown on to the flower patch and used as a fertiliser for roses or geraniums. That night a huge "borán" of turf was brought into the kitchen, and once more a roaring turf fire blazed in the hearth. After the rosary, a special word of thanks was slipped in - thanks be to God for giving us the means to be warm and cosy for another while. All of this lifting, carrying, pitching, throwing and picking was very hard physical work - I often wonder how much jogging done nowadays would equal the unloading of one load of turf?

Should a storm arise, and it very often did, the bádóirí and their boats were marooned at the pier, and had to "sit out the gale" and wait until it was safe to travel. These storms usually lasted only two days. However, I remember once the bad weather lasted a whole week and my mother sent us down with a basket - with a brown cake, a bottle of milk, a pat of homemade butter and a piece of bacon, from which they could cut rashers. The offering was thankfully received and a blessing passed on, "Abair le do mhama, go méadaí Dia a stór". "May God increase her store". Home we raced, thanking God that we didn't have to spend the night on that boat, bobbing like a cork on the rough and angry waters. I know for a fact that a bottle or two of the hot stuff - poitín - found their way to the loft in our kitchen and later to the reek of hay, the next time these bádóirí came by, their motto being that one good turn deserves another.

Very often, some of the bádóirí who came over on the turf boats stayed in Duras working on the farms. They were called Spailpíns or Spalpeens, and came especially for picking potatoes. They often worked full time with one farmer, but more often than not they worked a day here, two days there or wherever they got work. It was a hard life, but it could also be a happy one. Some of the men who came over, were very good-looking and strong and energetic and stole the hearts of the pretty girls living in the area. In spite of the romances, I cannot recall any of the men marrying and settling down. But I do remember that one bádóir made a match between his sister and a local man, and this was repeated by at least two others a few years later. Of course, there were many broken hearts when the Connemara lads decided to return home, minus their girlfriends, and they spring to mind when I hear the song "I'll forgive but I'll never forget". I also recall hearing a verse from a poem which was doing the rounds at the time.

"They came in boats, the spalpeen lads to labour on the land

They left behind some broken hearts and footprints in Trácht strand."

Trácht strand still remains as serene and idyllic as ever, waves ebbing and flowing as they have been doing from time immemorial, islands hazy in the distance, a tangy sea-weedy smell in the air, and seagulls wheeling and circling overhead, but the footprints have long since vanished.

But don't imagine that the hookers and pucáns just came over, emptied the turf and went back without a load. Indeed no. They took back provisions which were badly needed in their homes - potatoes, turnips, hay and lots of barley, for making poitín, no doubt. As well as that, housebuilding materials and timber for boat work were sent west by sea from Duras and Kinvara to Galway and Connemara. It was a kind of exchange trade, and a successful one too.

Later, much later, roads improved and lorries began to haul turf and gradually the boats stopped coming. So now, every year in Kinvara, Cruinniú na mBád - a festival of boating activities and re-enactment of the journey from

Connemara with loads of turf - takes place as a tribute to and commemoration of the bádóirí who so courageously manned the hookers, púcáns and gleoiteogs so many moons ago.

Led and said by religion

Religion played a major part in our lives, while we grew from babies into teens and into young women and men. It was a very natural and unquestioned part of everyday life. We just went along with whatever we were told. Even though, privately, we might complain and rail, publicly we endured in silence.

To say we were "led and said" by religion is an understatement. Everything done or said was overshadowed by religion. We were afraid of what the priests would say. We were afraid of what our parents would say. We were afraid of what the neighbours would say. We were afraid God would punish us. So we let the time for change pass us by and we let the time for discussion elapse.

Co-habiting - then unknown, at least in Duras - would probably have merited a witch hunt or a house burning. Sex education was a "sin". Indeed, the word "sex" was never spoken aloud among the grown-ups, and it was not encouraged in our childish vocabulary either. Questions were never asked openly. If you succeeded in voicing the question there was silence. Sex was mysterious, completely removed from us, remote, dangerous and, because of this, we, the curious ones, wanted to know more. As a child I ventured to ask where I came from and I was told, "You were found under a head of cabbage in the cabbage garden". Quite happily, I accepted this. We were conditioned to passive acceptance, and "no further questions". Later that spring, when I saw my father toiling in the cabbage garden, sowing plants which would eventually grow into heads of cabbage, I thought, there goes my father sowing shelters for new babies. Stirrings of questions were felt, but not followed through. I wouldn't dare. They were locked away in a haze of "taboo".

Married priests or women priests were two changes considered totally unworthy of the slightest consideration, so opinions were never voiced about them. Actually, the older people would turn in their graves if they knew of some of the "goings on" as we approach the end of the century. To them, and I suppose to us as well, a priest was a priest forever and was treated as a "man apart" - a man whose friendship should not be cultivated too closely just in case "temptation" reared its ugly head. The years have mellowed the strictness. Rules have been altered and somewhat softened, and what would have been viewed as heresy in my young days, is now totally acceptable or at least thinkable.

Receiving Holy Communion on the tongue was the only method of receiving when I was a child. Nobody, but nobody, ever touched the Host, only the priest. If by any mishap or unfortunate accident, the Host fell to the ground, then all surrounded the spot, motionless and in total silence. The priest took up the Host and put it away. Then he scrubbed the spot where it had fallen and everybody breathed again.

I saw this happen only once in my youth, but I got a lovely, caring feeling while we all surrounded the Host. We were now sheltering Him who shelters us every minute and hour of the day. Nowadays, the Host may be received in the hand, and transferred to the tongue. If it happens to fall, it is picked up without any "hullabaloo" and the service is continued. In the name of progress, and in the absence of sufficient priests, rules are relaxed, and "sticky" situations are viewed with less disapproval than they were when I was young.

Confessions once a month were a very definite "must" in the Duras of fifty years ago. Left to ourselves, we would have been happy to unburden ourselves less often, but parental control was such that once told to go, go you must. We really were hard put to find sins for every confession with the result that the same sins were told, re-cycled and re-told again and again, with a little "aguisín" added here and a "tail" knocked off there. I've no doubt but the good Lord got an immense amount of enjoyment out of our childish confessions. At least, we came and visited Him in his own home. It made no difference what news or stories we told him. In hindsight, that's how I like to think of my "confessional efforts". And I pray that the Heavenly Boss will agree with me!

Before leaving the subject, I must recount an hilarious story that did the rounds when I was young. Fr. Tom Burke, who was quite old by this time, travelled all over the parish in his pony and trap. The pony was well-trained and would stand outside the church, munching from an oats bag slung over his neck while his curate, Fr. Patrick Considine, sat inside in the confessional absolving the tit-bits told so confidentially and earnestly by the locals.

It so happened that one day the pony kicked the traces and strolled off down a boreen, barely wide enough for the pony, not to mention the trap. Pat Keane from Aughinish was cycling by when he spotted the pony and he immediately went into the church to tell the priest. He went into the confessional and related the news to Fr. Tom, who told him, "Go out and gently back out the pair of them, pony and trap, and I'll be out in a few minutes."

As Pat left the church, the priest stuck his head out of the confessional box and shouted after him, "Pat, if she refuses to budge, pat her on the rump, rub her neck, coax her, but whatever you do, don't knock her." Pat was as red as a beetroot as he made his way out of the church, past those who were waiting for their turn in the confessional.

It was a long time before he lived that story down, if, indeed, he ever did!

Whoever made the rule that we should fast from midnight before going to Holy Communion next day, must have been a man - a very strong, healthy, disciplined, strict, and rigid man, in fact, a martinet. It was one of the most difficult rules of all. Just imagine fasting from 7 or 8 o'clock on Saturday evening until Sunday morning at about 10.30 am - when 9 o'clock Mass would be well and truly over. Old people and children suffered most. I remember eating blackberries coming home from Mass, after a particularly long sermon - fada agus leadránach.

85

Thank God that this rule has been altered and I pray that the new rule of one hour is never abused. At all times I am an optimist, and it is my earnest hope that those who endured such harsh and severe measures as the all night fast will receive a greater degree of glory in Heaven - including myself of course!

Going to bed without saying the rosary was unthinkable. Indeed, you'd want to be "stretched and nearly dead" before being allowed to miss the nightly dedication. At a certain time every night, in every home in Duras, the rosary was recited. At school as children, my peers and I exchanged and compared notes and I discovered the piece of information that Rosary time was a nightly ritual. My father's beads always hung beside the arch on a nail over the fireplace. Every night, at the same time, he raised his hand, lifted off the beads, indicating in this silent, but authoritative, way that rosary time was here. Immediately, we all fell to our knees - family and visitors alike. We knelt against chairs but my mother never used any support. Once or twice, it did occur to me to remain seated and refuse to join the family circle - but knowing what the consequences would be, I just followed their example and prayed. The five decades were said, followed by the Hail, Holy Queen. Then my mother recited the litany, slowly and clearly and at the same speed every night. A long and seemingly endless list of prayers followed - for paternal and maternal relatives, for the souls in Purgatory, for the soul nearest to God, for the soul farthest from God, for the soul who had nobody to pray for him, for the neighbour who was sick, for good health, good weather and good crops. Prayers were said to thank God for the many goodnesses received - they were rarely itemised, only "bulked" - "for what you did last week" - such was their faith that they spoke as if He were there in the kitchen, as no doubt He was. Finally, the night prayer was said, while we crossed our arms over our chests and intoned:

"I must die; I do not know, when, where or how
But if I die in mortal sin, I am lost forever.
Sweet Jesus have mercy on me."

With that sobering thought, we ended the rosary and hoped that, for us and for our family, there would be a tomorrow, free from mortal sin.

Nowadays, you read that Mass attendance has fallen off, especially in urban areas. This certainly wasn't the case when I was growing up in Duras. Attendance was normally 100% and those who couldn't walk too well, made "provisions for a lift".

Linnanes in Parkmore had a side-car, and Farrells in Nogra had a trap. Those vehicles were enviously watched by us, as they trundled along the dusty road. How we longed for a lift! Once or twice, I "cadged" a lift by waiting until Linnane's sidecar was just passing our gate; then I raced out, and the driver, Tom Linnane, being the gentleman that he was, shouted "whoa" to the horse who tossed his head and snorted but did stop. I placed my foot on the driver's boot and up I was pulled to sit, high up on the box seat in front, and watched all the poor, weary pedestrians from my lofty perch. Occasionally, a farmer brought the common cart to Mass. He placed a "pleasure-board" across the well of the cart, from standard to standard, and up on this sat Mr and Mrs. Going to Mass meant so much to them that they went to untold lengths to get there.

I remember one old lady named Kate who took religion very seriously and who always arrived outside specified places long before time, in other words "miles too early". She was first outside the confessional on a Saturday and first outside the Church on Sunday. Once, when Patrick Huban passed by on a wet Sunday morning and saw her standing outside the Church, on one leg like a cailleach fhada, and a cruit with the cold, he said, "'Pon my word, Kate will get an awful cell if there's no Heaven". Perish the thought!

Even the Church building has changed since my first visit to the altar rails. For one thing, there are no altar rails now. Long ago we knelt down at the rails over which was placed a spotless white, lace-edged communion cloth. We put our hands under the cloth and held it under our chins to doubly ensure with the paten the safety of the Sacred Host. On leaving the altar we genuflected, right down until the knee thumped the ground. We walked down the church, hands joined, eyes downcast. Reverence and respect were the key words and I don't think we were lacking in either. Somebody would surely take you aside and admonish you if you swung your arms or strutted smilingly down the aisle. When you did something wrong, it was everybody's business and you were likely to get a good prod in the back and a thump on the arm.

Marriage in those days was for keeps. You picked your man or your woman, took your time over it and, whether you got a good bargain or not, you stuck with it. There was no place in the vocabulary for the terms 'incompatibility' or 'my own space' or 'changed my mind'. You did your work, reared your family and got on with your life. Maybe some people were unhappy and they surely were. But are they any happier now?

An ordinary sermon wasn't too bad every Sunday, but what we heard during a mission was unbelievable. "And if ye don't lead better lives, ye will be sorry forever. God will be angry. God will be very angry. So I tell you, say your prayers. Confess your mortal sins in Confession. Confess them often, because if you die in mortal sin, you'll go to hell for all eternity and eternity lasts forever and ever and ever . . ."

Each sentence, delivered in a loud aggressive voice, was accompanied by "thump, thump, thump" on the sides of the pulpit. All the while, the priest grew redder and redder in the face, and really worked himself into a rage.

This is one of my earliest memories of the Missioners - and I must admit not a very happy one. A mission was held every few years, and specially trained priests came pontificating to us - the sinners. They frightened the living daylights out of us - well, out of me, in particular. I thought of God as a very cross missioner who saw and knew everything, everybody, everywhere - but yet didn't seem to care that we poor people were doing our level best to be friends with him. The missioners, God bless them, seemed to preach and shout at their congregations. Nowadays, we are told it's very difficult to commit a mortal sin. Back in my young days, everything we did seemed to be a sin. I remember at one mission, we were told that if we kept on committing sins, and displeasing God, "a tidal wave would come and carry us all out to sea". I honestly believed this and spent many sleepless nights wondering "will the tidal wave come tonight?" And when I questioned my mother, she said, "Sure, he didn't mean it at all." - "Ha, Ha", said I to myself, "so priests tell lies too". And I never could discover what sins could the people of my parish ever commit that would merit drowning by a tidal wave.

I remember that I was petrified of hell, and so were all of my school friends. I most certainly did not want to go to hell, so I went off to Confession every month and really bent the priest's ear telling my sins. To be honest, when I couldn't remember any sins - something which occurred now and again - I invented some, and once the priest almost fell out of the confessional in disbelief when I told him, "I told lies 1,000 times. I was bold 800 times" and instead of stopping me, he just said "Anything else?" And in my innocence, I thought that if God knew the good things as well as the bad things, the scales of justice might weigh in my favour, so I usually added a postscript, "Dear Lord, I always said my prayers and I never missed Mass".

There were two priests sharing the work of Kinvara and Duras parishes. One was old and very deaf, one was younger. The story was that those who had "hairy" sins went to the deaf man, rattled off a long list and were absolved. He didn't hear one word they said.

At that time, going to confessions was a terrifying experience. The confessional stood in isolation in the Church and the penitents knelt all around it. You just took your place in the line and knelt down to wait your turn. You examined your conscience as best you could, made out a long list and promptly forgot them. In spite of yourself, you listened to the whispers in the confessional. You also listened to the gurglings and rumblings of the stomachs. You shuffled your feet, you coughed. You rattled your beads. You coughed again - but still the whispers and gurglings continued, and persisted. One by one, the penitents went in, whispered, were shouted at, whispered again and came out with red faces half hidden by shawls or scarfs or maybe turned shamefully away. They then walked up the church and said whatever penance was given by the confessor. When I sat or knelt

89

in the line, as my turn came nearer I grew more nervous, more fearful, more agitated and kept repeating my long list of sins and their numbers over and over again, until they ended in a "mixum gatherum".

Several times, while waiting, I contemplated flight but seeing my mother praying at the end of the seat, I knew I would be hauled back, so I stayed where I was. After a little while, the person in front of me disappeared into the darkness of the confessional and I was next. My heart raced and then slowed. My mouth got dry. My hands perspired and there was a singing sensation in my ears and long before I entered the box I was a nervous wreck. Once inside, my eyes became accustomed to the darkness and I stared at the shutter. I could hear the undertones of the priest as he spoke to the person on the opposite side - and then with a shattering noise, the shutter was pulled across. I nearly always fell to pieces, forgot the confiteor, missed out on how long since my last good confession, blurted out my sins, and wouldn't you know - mixed them all up. I spoke in a whisper and almost collapsed when the priest said, "Speak up" - so I had to start all over again, and what I forgot, I invented. May the Omniscient Lord forgive me for ever having thought of Him as a cross missioner. I now know Him to be a gentle, kind and merciful God, eager to help me, only waiting for me to ask. When the Act of Contrition time came, I raced through it and triumphantly shouted "Amen".

By this time the priest usually had pulled the shutter and, once again, I was in darkness. Then I made my way through the kneeling people who looked at me as though I had killed somebody. On reaching a seat in the middle of the church, I discovered I couldn't remember my penance, so in a forlorn hope that I might hit the right one, I said all the penances I could think of - Hail Marys, Our Fathers, a decade of the rosary, hail Holy Queens - vowing to listen more carefully next time.

Once, a very funny situation occurred in the Confessional. A brother and sister, Paddy Gardiner and Bridie, went in, one on either side. Both shutters were open and sister and brother stared across at each other. Paddy made all kinds of faces at Bridie as she told her sins until eventually she got a fit of the giggles. The priest promptly cleared her off the premises, predicting that all kinds of bad things would happen to her - until he turned around and saw Paddy's grinning face. Him, he promptly cleared as well and when telling the story afterwards, the priest said, "I closed both shutters and sat in the darkness to compose myself, more convinced than ever that there are two sides to every story".

Confessions nowadays are comparatively painless. No matter how bad the sin, no matter how grave, no matter how often committed - absolution and forgiveness are forthcoming and readily given by the priest. However, in my young days, one of the greatest disincentives to sin was the fact that to get pardon, I'd have to tell the priest and he would surely shout and give out and everybody could hear. So, in order to make sure that we didn't get screamed at, we just didn't commit the sins. As good a reason as any I imagine. I'm sorry to say that the priests of that time were not very helpful, or didn't have time to listen to a child's "sceilín", or weren't like the batteries, 'ever ready' to give absolution and, in hindsight, perhaps they were responsible for the dislike, fear and distrust my peers and I have for the confession box.

Religion certainly occupied a very central place in our lives. Religious practices and customs were accepted as integral things to be done. Garland Saturday night was a night on which a pattern was held. It was the last Saturday in July and on that evening pilgrims left their homes and walked to St. Kieran's bed in Tracht. It was not really a bed, just a statue of St. Kieran set up in a sheltered part of Farrell's field, in a little valley. The imprint of a knee in the stone beside the statue, lent veracity to the story that this saint had prayed there. The pilgrims came there either in petition or in thanksgiving. There were certain prayers and rosaries to be said while walking slowly round the bed, and then you bent your knee in the imprint and made your request or thanked God for a cure. And several people were cured, so there was always a steady stream of people praying there on that particular weekend, and the majority of them slept there overnight and went to Duras Mass on Sunday morning.

But we youngsters heard a different story about the pilgrimage, and it appealed very much to us. If you were looking for a man and the job was proving more difficult than expected, not to worry, help was at hand. A visit to St. Kieran's bed was recommended and some conditions had to be fulfilled. First you said the rosary in private or aloud – it didn't really matter. The majority of visitors preferred to say it privately as they hoped to get more rapid results. Then you hopped around the statue three times, saying at the same time "Holy St. Kieran and Blessed St. Anne, send me a man as quick as you can". The hopping began at the knee imprint and continued for three rounds on the same leg without stopping. Having done that, if you had any energy left you bent your knee to the count of three in the imprint of the saint's knee. Finally, you wrapped your shawl or coat tightly around you and slept there for the night. Looking back at the number of women who "did" the pattern every Garland Saturday night, I often wondered did they get their men? Or were they there for a cure or a thanksgiving?

Once my father saw an advanced lady of about 60 years on her way to St. Kieran's bed and he said, "What in the name of God is that hairpin going looking for a man for...." So women of all ages must have done the pattern because hope springs eternal in the human breast.

Did it work? I hear you ask. Well, for me it didn't - aged about 10 years, I went down to the field and having made sure nobody was looking, I raced through the rosary, hopped and recited, bent my knee to the count of three and fled. I ran all the way home half expecting the man to appear round every corner, but it was many years later before St. Kieran got around to answering my prayer, with a little help from myself!

Religion actually spawned a phraseology all of its own. Every sentence was interspersed with Thanks be to God, or Please God or God between us and all harm, or even May God forgive me. Religious terminology was accepted norm, and very often a person was assessed on the number of sentences used having God thrown in somewhere. Occasionally, a man could develop a habit of saying I declare to God or God knows or, as my own father used to say, good God Almighty, but that was really frowned on, and was not considered good manners.

So, religion continued to lead us but the clergy were, for

us, an unknown quantity. The local priest never visited the homes at all, but he did visit the school where he sat on a chair and expounded high powered catechetics and then threw questions at us and was staggered when we couldn't answer them. The Bishop we only saw once every three years, because that's how often we had confirmation. We had learned our catechism from cover to cover, could recite all the miracles and parables, could explain transubstantiation and could say endless prayers in English and Irish, but one look at this prince of the church and all the information vanished. His entrance into the crowded silent-as-a-grave church, struck terror into our hearts. He projected a lofty, grand, untouchable figure; a person so far removed from us that we were sure he didn't even breathe the same air. This image of course had a disastrous effect on impressionable youngsters, and the memory I have of my one and only meeting with him is not exactly a happy one. My sister, Julia, and I and our classmates were being confirmed and were in Duras church for the pre-confirmation catechism examination which took place the evening before the actual confirmation day. We were herded into the church at 2 o'clock for the 3 o'clock arrival of the Bishop and his entourage. He didn't arrive until four and then made his way up the aisle, finally facing us haughtily as we sat cringing in our seats. Julia and I were dressed alike – two white dresses with lace collars and blue satin ribbons around our necks, waiting to receive our medals next day. We had blue bows in our hair, and black hornpipe shoes. The dreaded moment came and the Bishop stood in front of Julia. "What is Holy Orders?", he asked her. She answered in a frightened voice and he moved to me. "What is Extreme Unction?", he said while his eyes darted back to Julia and then returned to me. I finished and there was silence. "Are you two...sisters?", he asked in his distinctly nasal voice. "Yes, my Lord", I croaked, wishing the ground would swallow me. "Are you two...twins?", he enquired indicating Julia and I with the slightest of head nods. "No, my Lord", I whispered through convulsive throat constrictions. And he moved on.

My father, who was down at the back of the church, said afterwards, "You should have said, 'No, my Lord, we are not twins, but we are Quinns'". This was my one and only brush with our Bishop.

In retrospect, everything we did and said was under the religious umbrella. "Tomorrow, we'll make the hay, please God. God forgive you for telling a lie. Don't forget to go to Confession on Sunday. I've eaten too much for dinner, may God forgive me. I saw that man with one eye, the Lord between us and all harm. Johnny's father is dead, the Lord have mercy on his soul. That was a lovely supper, thank God". The very conversation was littered with God and things belonging to God, and without any doubt, we were led and said by religion, not because it was something we wanted, but because it was in the times, and you went *with* the times, not against them.

Wealth from the sea

Duras is situated beside the sea, on an inlet of Galway Bay. Standing in Tracht on any clear night, the Galway lights could be seen winking and blinking across the bay. They were a tantalising reminder that another life existed out there, a life at which we, having been reared in the confines of a poor village, could only guess. Again, while standing in Tracht, one could see clearly Island Eddy to the right, on which, at that time, many families lived. Like many another island, it is now uninhabited and homes which once re-echoed to calls from children and animals are now silent and overgrown.

To the left one could get a glimpse of Deer Island, away on the horizon like a tiny black dot. On a clear day, it could be seen quite easily but on a misty, foggy day it was shrouded in mystery and seemed to disappear off the face of the earth. Later on, I'll tell about my visit to the lonely island and the almost disastrous results. It was, of course, uninhabited.

The sea, which my father used to say "should never be trusted", delivered many of its riches to us with relatively no bother. Each farmer who owned land, owned a portion of shore as well. The seaweed on this shore was cut and used as fertilizer on the crops. Spreading seaweed was a job nobody wanted but one which was very necessary. The seaweed was spread as manure on the drills of slits using a four-pronged fork. It seeped its goodness down through the clay and the results were rich healthy crops of potatoes – Epicures, Aran Banners, Kerr Pinks and Golden Wonders. Sometimes, the farmer sold a few lorries of seaweed to Kilrush for bone meal or calf meal and iodine. When the weed was dried, it was called múrach and was used as manure. These lorries of seaweed were sold to inland farmers in Kiltartan, Gort, Ardrahan, Kilbeacanty or Loughrea. The night after the sale, all of the immediate details of the farmer and his family were related by my father to whomever was willing to listen as they sat around the fire. Very often the person who bought the seaweed might be met again at a fair in Kinvara or Gort, and the two farmers renewed a friendship, all because of a lorry load of weed which had changed hands for one pound or thirty bob. My sister, Mary, told me that once, at a dance in Labane, a young man asked her out to dance. After his initial shyness had worn off, he informed her that he had once visited our house with his father to buy weed and that later "Both of our fathers had bought pigs from the same cart". So, tiny threads spread out through widespread communities, and pulled relationships together and linked lives from places which then were considered far apart.

The sea was a generous provider of fish of all shapes and sizes. People caught herring, mackerel and trout. Some farmers had currachs and one or two had fishing boats, complete with sails. The boat belonging to Willie Shaughnessy was the one I was most familiar with. When herring were plentiful and too many were caught, the bean an tí dried them and kept them for later. First, she gutted them, cleaned and washed them and flattened them out. Then she hung them on the clothes line to dry in the sun for a day or two. Finally, sundried and golden brown, they were rubbed with fine salt and were saved in barrels. They were absolutely tasty and eaten with relish when bad weather prevented any fishing being done. Then the barrel would be opened up and the fish eaten, and they tasted like kippers - only much better.

We were no strangers to shellfish either, yielded up in abundance by the ever-generous sea. We picked bairneachs, diúilicíns, faocháin and sceanna mara. The latter were devious creatures and very sensitive to sound. The minute they heard somebody walking across the sand and sensed the approaching vibrations, they swiftly sidled down deep into the sandy darkness and would have to be dug out. You had to be very quick to get the spade down under them, as they kept moving down deeper and deeper. When the fish were eaten, the children used the empty shells as knives in our little make believe houses, and the large cockle shells as dishes. God between us and all harm, weren't we easily entertained! All of this seafood was cooked in different ways, and I have yet to eat it in any restaurant tasting as good as it tasted in our country kitchen long ago, when hunger was gnawing at the "insides". And, of course, we all know that hunger is the best sauce! Nowadays in the "in" restaurants, these fish of far off days are named on the menu as limpets, mussels, periwinkles and razor fish, choice seafood and expensive items indeed. My mother had a special recipe for cooking mussels, which she served up with a white sauce and surrounded by mashed potatoes, it was simply delicious. I only wish I had paid more attention to her when she was cooking, and devoured the method as well as the end product.

The rocks, covered and uncovered daily by the sea, held more than seaweed. They also held cairigín or carrageen moss, a yellowy plant-like seaweed, only edible. It was collected off the rocks, by hand. You grabbed, and pulled, and stuffed into a bag – very hurtful on the lámha or hands, I must say. The bags were brought home and the cairigín was spread out on the grass until the sun bleached it white. Then it was turned over and whitened underneath. When thoroughly dry and crisp, it was packed into dry bags and sold to buyers who came to Duras and now and again to Kinvara to buy. The Gibbons brothers from Mayo were the biggest buyers of the moss. They came to Duras very often - to the cross at Nogra where all the locals gathered with their bags. They bought it by weight when completely dry, and weighed it there where everybody could see. Once, I saw an old man opening his two bags and sprinkling them from a can of water. When I enquired what he was at, he calmly told me he was "just sprinkling a few drops of holy water to guide them on their way". Of course, he was dampening them and by doing so was adding to their weight.

On doing some research on the uses of cairigín moss, I discovered that some of it was sent to France where it was used by cosmetic and pharmaceutical firms to make gels and cough mixtures. But most of the moss was sold to

English breweries where it was used to make beer clear. It seems that beer was poured through the moss and all impurities and imperfections went into the moss and were held there, while the beer flowed clear and clean. I'm sure that cairigín moss has out-lived its use in that area in the present year.

Once a crowd of us young people - we were about fifteen or sixteen years - borrowed his fishing boat from Willie Shaughnessy and, with Kitty Hynes who was a wonderful sea woman, we headed for Deer Island. It was a bright, sunny summer's day and the sea was as calm as a mirror. The abiding memory I have of the island is the number of birds - seagulls especially. We "parked" the boat and set to work with a will. The carrageen was plentiful and in no time at all we had the bags full and the tide turned and we were on our way home. It was now getting late in the evening and the sky had turned a dark, menacing dull grey. Gusts of wind sent the boat scurrying across the bay. We passed Tracht and had to round a bend called Craicneach, with very deep and treacherous waters.

Suddenly, the boat seemed to lurch and kind of keeled over. The wind was now quite strong. Kitty was magnificent and did something with ropes and sails and righted it. We were all silent as we felt "this is it". Kitty shouted at us to bail, as the boat was leaking and the rim barely above the water. Suddenly we saw Willie - good old Willie - on the rocks, cupping his hands round his mouth and shouting, "Toss out the bags and let down half a sail". So out went our hard earned bags - all twenty of them and Kitty lowered a sail and the boat sort of limped into Parkmore Pier. We jumped out and raced back along the shore to retrieve the bags and then headed for home.

My father was cycling down the road to meet us and by the scowl on his face, I knew he was both angry and relieved. My mother was fussing over me and her comment was, "Thank God, your time hasn't come yet". But it was an adventure I wouldn't care to repeat, and only for Kitty, not one of us adventurous young people would have lived to tell the tale.

Carrageen was used as dessert or, as we used to say, "as pudding". Indeed, it is still, according to present day standards, quite a desirable item on any menu. It was made with milk and while still hot, nutmeg or cinnamon was sprinkled on the top. When cold it was mouth watering and when hot was very soothing for a sore throat.

Duileasc or dilisk was another edible sea plant, reddish in colour and pretty strong tasting. For some unknown reason, it never really "got off the ground". Smugairlí róin or jellyfish were in profusion but were only known for the sharp stings which they delivered, silently and stealthily.

The sea, which could just as easily have been our enemy, was undoubtedly our very good friend. It also gave us a safe, tranquil beach on which we swam, where we walked and collected shells, or where we just sat and watched the fish, the birds and the endless waves, crashing or lapping gently on the shore. By the way, Tracht still remains a lovely, slightly remote beach, over which St. Kieran's statue watches. Many years ago, this statue was erected in Tracht, donated by Mrs Curtin of Currenrue, and it still stands. Kieran was a very holy man living in the Aran Islands with his monks. He wished to cross to Duras but had no boat and no hope of getting one. So he knelt and prayed and the waters opened and left a dry road all the way to Tracht strand. Led by St. Kieran, the monks, holy men and students crossed over in single file, with the walls of water each side. As St. Kieran stepped ashore in Tracht, he discovered that he had forgotten his prayer book. He told the man behind him, who in turn told the man behind him and this continued until the last man, just leaving Aran, heard the news. He, of course, took the book and handed it to Kieran on his arrival in Tracht. They are supposed to have spent a couple of days and nights there, days fishing and praying and nights sleeping and praying. St. Kieran blessed the waters and prayed that they would always contain fish and to spare. Because of this, the statue was built and he presides over the strand.

For men may come and men may go
But the sea goes on forever.

Mike - a village tragedy

Mike was a loner. He lived alone and died alone. He was very poor, as indeed many were around that time. He was born in 1880 and lived all his life in his little home in Duras. It was a one bedroomed building with a kitchen off it. He had a horse and a few hens, and that was about all.

Mike was poor and got assistance from neighbours – assistance, I must say, for which he never asked but was happy to accept. They all knew when he was in want. Farrells and Fahys, who owned the local shops, never refused him goods on "tick" and each shop gave him Christmas goods for nothing. All the neighbouring women, Molly, Maggie, my mother and Delia, gave willingly and generously. Any day we'd see Mike foraging in the bushes in the field across the road and on hearing this, my mother, ever alert to the needs of those less fortunate than herself, would fill a bottle of milk and cut a quarter of a brown cake and send one of us out to give it to him. Two days later, he'd appear with a dozen small wild red apples - juicy, sweet and deliciously edible. "Mike is proud", said my mother, "and he likes to feel that he is paying back something for what we give him. Poor Mike, he is so alone". He called to Molly Sullivan, who gave him a piece of bacon and maybe a few potatoes. He called to Maggie Hynes, who gave him tea and listened to him. But he never went to Mass. Nobody ever knew why or at what particular time he stopped visiting the Lord's house. He told my mother once that he "couldn't bear crowds" or the thought of being "hemmed in". However, that didn't interfere with his daily prayers or "chats" as he called them. He prayed very often, every day and especially on

Sunday. Once I heard him saying "God is never too busy to listen to me" and we said, "But how do you know that he listens to you?" "Because", he said, "he always answers me". But what went on between Mike and his maker remains a mystery.

It happened over a long weekend - when a holy day of obligation fell on Monday. It was summer time and people were busy. Visitors were passing to Tracht and Masses had to be attended. It was Tuesday before somebody voiced the concern that "Mike is missing", because his horse was found straying on the road. Nobody had seen him for days and the news spread like wildfire. This news in such a closeknit community caused great alarm and greater feelings of guilt. How could this have happened? Why didn't somebody notice? Why were we all so self-engrossed that we hadn't a minute to spend worrying about Mike?

All the men gathered together in Mike's street - John Fahy, Pat Sullivan, Martin and Patrick Hynes, Tommy Kilkelly, Mike Farrell and Mattie, Michael Carty, Tom Linnane and my father. They called his name, "Mike, are you there? Can you hear us?", but no voice answered, no whisper whispered, not even a bird twittered. All was as silent as the grave. By now, the group was anxious, tense and tight. They walked around calling Mike's name but got no answer, heard no voice and saw nothing. Later, John Fahy said, "It was as if everything and everybody waited with baited breath".

Finally, a decision was taken that somebody should go in through the window. My father was chosen because he was a small man and could just about squeeze in through the tiny aperture which served as a window. The whole window was taken out and in went my father. His screech of dismay and gasp of horror were enough to convey to the waiting men outside that something was terribly wrong. As indeed it was. Actually, my father was not himself for many months afterwards, as the awful sight which met his eyes had indelibly etched itself on his mind.

Mike lay on the floor, quite dead. His toes were eaten, as were his ears and nose, by rats and mice who now inhabited the kitchen. His hair was infested with crawling

101

lice and his teeth were bared in a painful grimace of death. His open eyes were blind and his dark blue fingers were clutching his throat. He was sprawled half under the table with one leg screwed up under his body. It was an awful sight and one which transfixed my father for a minute; then he pulled back the bolt to allow the others to come in and recited the act of contrition in Mike's half eaten ear. A clean sheet was got from Molly who cried, "ochon, ochon, poor Mike, may God and Mike forgive us". It was a shattering crisis to the villagers. A man had died alone, without help or comfort from any human being, and each person felt that he should have been there. They were poor, hardworking, God-fearing people and had pity and to spare for their fellowmen. Anyhow, a messenger was dispatched to Kinvara to ask the doctor and the priest to call. While they waited, the men recited the rosary as my father said afterwards. "not really for Mike, but for all ourselves as well".

Soon, Doctor Connolly arrived, black bag dangling, gold pocket watch straining across an ample tummy, breath coming flutteringly from a button mouth. A kind man he was, and a man who was used to seeing death in all shapes and forms, but on seeing Mike, he was dumbfounded and visibly shaken. Added to the sight was the stench, that stale smell of death which makes a person gag and gasp. He gave his hat to my father and then proceeded to examine the remains, glasses low on his nose, eyes narrowed to mere slits. After a short time, he tut-tutted and shook his head. "Exposure and heart, and maybe two days he's dead. I'll certify this and may God have mercy on him", he said. Out in the fresh air, he gulped in some badly needed oxygen and wiped his sweating forehead. "A sad business this", he said, "death is lonely at the best of times, but death without company is twice as lonely", and away he went.

The priest came and with stern face and eyes that missed nothing, he entered the kitchen. Looking on the human remains of poor, dead, Mike, he raised his hands and implored a merciful God to forgive him his sins and deal with him lightly. He ended by reciting the Our Father rather quickly and rushed out into the air equally as quickly. When he had regained his composure, he eyed the men and said, "Mike hasn't been to Mass for years and this means he has broken the third commandment. So, for this reason, he'll get no rest in the church tonight. It's best if he is buried straight away". Now these villagers were terribly shocked at this news, and some grew pale. They had never heard the like and didn't think Mike deserved this harsh treatment. After all, from time immemorial wasn't it always usual to leave the corpse in the church for a last visit before Mass next morning and then burial. To deprive Mike of this little "cuairt" was very frightening and caused some consternation. The men shuffled and whispered and finally someone said, "Please let us bring him to the church for a couple of hours", but he was sharply reprimanded by the priest who by now was angry and cross, "You'll do as I say", he boomed, "and remember, I'm the boss. It's near three now. Take him and bury him straight away."

Tom Fahy was commissioned to nail together a plain timber coffin which received Mike's body wrapped in Molly's white sheet. Nonie Fahy wound her good beads round his poor mutilated fingers and a bottle of holy water was left in by his side by Mary Farrell. The coffin was closed and lifted onto a bed of straw in the back of my father's cart, drawn by our big, hairy-legged plough horse. The small, sad, lonely procession moved off down the road. I remember it patchily, but didn't understand it too well. My mother cried silently, great big fat tears rolling down her cheeks - and all the other local women had the same reaction, a guilty feeling that Mike should have slipped away without their prior knowledge and a feeling of shame that they had allowed it to happen.

The coffin moved round the car, but was gently pushed back in to safety. Hands were left on it to keep it steady and to give the impression that they were giving strength and support to what was left of Mike's earthly remains. Horse, cart, coffin and men moved off down the road past the Mash, past the windmill, past Geata Árd and to the right to Parkmore graveyard. A grave had been hastily dug in a corner of the graveyard near shifting sands, and there the coffin was carried and lowered by willing hands. The crowd by now had increased as word had gotten 'round and all the homes in the locality were represented. Tom and Sean Fahy, John and Patrick Connors, Pete Bohannon, John Melody, Tommy Moloney, Pat and Sonny Sullivan, Denny and Mike Hynes, Mick Linnane, John Glynn, Thomas Mooney - all standing silently round the open grave, heads bowed, hats and caps off. No priest came to say a last prayer or offer a plea of leniency. Mike didn't deserve such treatment simply because he had transgressed by non-attendance at Mass. But we young people argued in later years when we had a discussion about Mike. Surely Mike's sin, if it was a sin, was known by everybody? What about the unknown sins, what about the millions of sins committed in private? "What about them?". My mother used to say, "Don't be judgemental". Anyhow, the general opinion was that Mike had been badly treated and that, instead of praying for him, we should all pray to him.

This village tragedy brought shadows of mortality into our lives and showed us that nobody is exempt from death. Here was Mike among us one day, living, breathing, enjoying a quality of life such as it was. Next day, he was struck down, gone and all but forgotten. A month later, as we passed the graveyard, Julia and I jumped in to look at the grave. There was a rectangular piece of ground with green grass growing profusely over it and only for the wooden cross to mark the spot, there was nothing to show that Mike ever was. So was the transcience of life demonstrated to us.

Every November, when the Holy souls envelope has to be filled with names of our dead, I always start the list with the name Mike Niland and I hope and pray that he will remember me in his happy home with his Friend at last.

Round the house
and mind the dresser

S pecial social occasions were few and far between
when I was growing up and because of their scarcity
they were more thoroughly enjoyed. They were
talked about in shivering anticipation for a week
beforehand, and they were nattered about with happy
memories for two weeks afterwards.

The house hooley or the céilí was what most caught our
fancy. These dances were held in the home - some
families needed no excuse and just held them at "the drop
of a hat". If it happened that a member of the family
played a musical instrument, so much the better. The
stone kitchen floor was swept clean. The stools, forms and
few kitchen chairs were pushed back tightly against the
white-washed walls. One good solid chair - one that
wasn't 'bacach' or didn't have bacadaigh legs - was set up
in the middle of the table for the musician. This was done
so he wouldn't be shoved or pushed or elbowed by the
dancers when the half sets began.

My cousin, Mattie Quinn in Geeha, was a marvellous
melodeon player. His home was the ideal place for a
hooley. The huge kitchen had a solid stone floor. There
was a resident musician and many young family members
- all the ingredients for a lively céilí. There were never any
invitations. Nobody was ever invited and nobody was
ever turned away. The house was always full. Being
cousins, we girls always heard about the hooley well in
advance, and had plenty of time to get ready.

Not that it made any difference because getting ready
only took a minute or two. There was no make-up to be

put on. You relied on nature. Looking back, it seems to me that what we wore didn't matter; rather the personality, gaiety and friendliness of the person did. Speaking for myself, I remember I had only two good dresses and I must have washed and worn them to death. Nevertheless at a ceili I never left the floor, and I was never short of a partner.

In retrospect, it seems that I, third in the family, was brought along to ceilis at a very young age. My father had his own reason for doing this. If he wished, he could go home early and plead my extreme youth as an excuse. Sometimes, when it was time to go to the ceili, my father often "baulked" and said he was too tired, or that it looked like rain or . . . So we begged, pleaded and cajoled and usually won.

Off we set, walking maybe two miles. Sometimes you might be offered a lift on the bar of a bicycle - this was most uncomfortable and a hazard because a dress could easily get caught in the spokes and be ruined, so very often walking was the better choice. Not even the rain deterred us once we got it into our heads; we were "rarin" to go. Our excitement grew as we marched up the road, over the boreen, out on the Cloosh road, gathering other céilí goers on our way.

To this day, I can remember standing at the gate of Quinns, the ceili house, listening to the music as it was carried through the open kitchen door. Light streamed out from a large oil lamp which would cost a fortune nowadays. Shadows came and went on the shaded windows as the dancers kicked up their heels to the "Connacht Man's Rambles", or "A Trip to the Cottage". We crowded into the already crowded kitchen and, as we were good dancers, were immediately claimed by other good dancers. Oh! What rhythm! What bliss! What sheer animal delight as we pounded the floor in the half set, the stack of barley or the waltz. When a barn dance was called, off we went, "Toe, heel 1-2-3, Round the house and mind the dresser", the dance ending in a double swing and much laughter. There was a lady called Nora Sullivan who could dance the barn dance as nobody else could, so we all gradually moved back and let her take the floor. And, my goodness, but she could dance and hop and hit the floor in spots, just like a top.

A good dancer could be busy all night, asked for the next dance and the next one and the one after that. The rule was that, if a man asked you to dance, you usually accepted. If a man danced well, that was an added bonus and you could afford to ignore the bald head, or the whiskey nose, or even the beer belly, in the delight of matching steps and enjoying the rhythm.

However, there were certain types to be avoided and sidestepped. Word would filter through the crowd that "so and so" had travelling hands. They travelled up and down, back and forth across the back - and elsewhere, if allowed.

Having been warned, it was then up to each girl to make sure she didn't dance with him. You tried not to make eye contact with him at all costs, so he could not "beckon" to you. When he approached, you disappeared. When he reappeared, you ducked and sat in the hob until the coast was clear once more. If, however, he happened to "nab" you, you'd just have to dance and "suffer on".

Another type who could put a damper on the night was "the snorer". This fellow usually asked you out for the waltz - "The Rose of Mooncoin" or "When it's Moonlight in Mayo" - "nothing wrong with that", sez you. Once on the floor, he promptly fell asleep on your shoulder and snored. He waltzed around the kitchen as if by instinct, snoring or breathing quite loudly. You did you best to talk to him, but he was oblivious. Soon, however, all the young dancers rallied round and bumped and nudged your man awake. You escaped as soon as possible, and had a good laugh.

But you could very easily go from the frying pan into the fire and fall into the clutches of the "whistler". This man shuffled up to the end of the kitchen, turned at the headland, and shuffled down again, all the time whistling his own music and what's more, dancing to it. He stepped it out to his own tune, while you stepped it out to the tune from the melodeon. If both could step and hop at the same time, the result would not be too bad. But it happened that ye went bumpety-bump, ouch! sore ankles, and sorer toes and a vow on your part - never again! However, these types didn't put a damper on the enjoyment of the night. Rather, they added a challenge.

During a hooley, the floor could be swept two or three times, and very often a dash of water was sprayed on "to keep the dust down". This caused a lull in the dancing and singers were recruited and called on to "give a verse or two" or "cough up a stave of a song". Some very good singers would entertain the crowd with the lovely old songs like "On the shores of Americay", which was normally sung by Mary Quinn-Marshall. And while she was singing, you could hear a pin drop. "Noreen Bawn" was another general favourite and so was "The Crúiscín Lan", sung always by Mary Hynes Duane. I've never heard anybody sing it as well as she did. Sarah Linnane Hynes used to sing "I'll forgive but I'll never forget" so feelingly that we'd have tears in our eyes. When the men sang, they did so loudly, kept their eyes shut and rocked back and forth to lend emphasis to the words. My father, who wasn't a bad singer at all, would sing "Nora Daly" or "Peigin Leitir Mhor" - ar an sean nós. He might also dance a jig and create his own steps as he went on, and clap for himself when he'd finish.

At about this time, windows would be opened for air, and some young "daft" lads would go outside, push a stick through the open window and "fish" a cap or a hat off some unsuspecting heads. Such innocent fun! Once I saw my father's hat being lifted off his head, and ever so slowly being pulled out the window, but the stick broke, the hat fell and my father reclaimed it amid great laughter and shaking of fists.

Suddenly, it would be time for tea. Brewed in two or three large enamel teapots and left sitting in the ashes for a few seconds, it tasted absolutely great. It was accompanied by currant or raisin bread cut in "canndaí", thick slices of apple cake, and sometimes homemade buns. Very often, if the crowd was unusually large and hungry, the sweet cakes were quickly devoured and then "the grinder" was cut into slices and plastered with butter. Yarns were told, and funny incidents recalled and embroidered. Soon, the music restarted and dancing recommenced - even livelier and with more gusto than before, as all the batteries had been recharged by the tea-break.

Often, to our horror, my father's eagle eye would spot the grandfather clock and he would "round us up" for departure. In vain, we begged him to stay another while and his answer was always the same, "Sure it would suit ye fine to stay up all night and in bed all day". With that, we knew he would not change his mind and so we called thanks to the bean an tí, and to the musician, winked laughingly at the young man who had been whispering sweet nothings all night, and headed for home. We lingered in the doorway for a last eyeful of the crowded, once again dusty kitchen, the nodding fear an tí on the hob, and the by-now dying kitchen fire. We always really hated to leave. The walk home was never a walk, but a brisk trot. Looking up at the stars, my father would say "All decent people should be in bed by now", but we youngsters were very happy to be among the indecent ones who were still up.

On my last visit to America in March 1990, I spent hours talking to a "gamelty" of Irish, living in Norwood, Hartfort and Connecticut at whose homes those ceilis were held so long ago. We recalled those happy nights and relived many of the céilís, and the general consensus was "How simple and thoroughly enjoyable it all was, and how we danced with glee to the tune of "Round the house and mind the dresser", so many moons ago". Simple treats for simple folk.

"It's poitín you devil"

Poitín was a "master" drink or, as my father used to say, "a cure for all ills". It found its way to Duras by means of the turf boats. These boats sailed from Connemara to the Parkmore pier and the bádóirs usually brought over a few bottles with them. Poitín was the local home-made whiskey, brewed in stills in the bogs of Connemara. It was a colourless liquid, and looked just like water - you'd know whether it was water or not when you took a "swig of it"! And one swig was enough. Indeed, oftentimes a man could get drunk on one swallow - depending on how long it lasted - the swallow I mean. Once I saw a man having a go at a bottle. He raised it to his mouth, and his Adam's apple bobbed up and down four or five times before he took the bottle away, wiped his mouth with the back of his hand and said, "'Pon my soul, I could get used to that".

Bottles of poitín could be bought from the bádóirs, but the buyers and the sellers had to be very wary as poitín was an illegal drink. The gardaí were always on the look out, but were seldom lucky. The bottle of poitín could be stored either in the loft over the kitchen, or deep in the reek of hay. Once I saw my father sinking his arm in the hay stack, right up to his "oxter" or arm pit, then he walked away satisfied. Needless to say, when he was out of sight I, too, sank my arm and felt the bottle - enough said. At that time, the farmers tied down the reeks of hay with ropes and weighed them down with heavy stones. Well, these stones were the landmarks and as many as four bottles could be safely stashed away and preserved for an occasion, right beside the stones. Gardai could come and gardai could go, but they could never find the hiding places.

Sometimes they moved the bottles, when word got round that the gardai were on the warpath. One morning early, I saw my father briskly trotting down the road with two bottles under his oxters. He had already tied some strings on to them and he continued on down to the "Mash", where the tide came in every evening. He hung the bottles on the bridge wall and let them slide down into the water. Then he secured the strings around some stones. There the bottles remained until the hullabaloo had died down. Who'd ever think of searching there?

As well as drinking poitín, it could also be used as a medication to rub on the body. Now that I come to think of it, women rarely used it, men always did. My father suffered a lot from rheumatism and had great "faith" in a rub of poitín. One morning, he had just started rubbing some on his leg when Tom Fahy walked in - straight into the kitchen as everybody did at that time. He stood inside the door and raised his head, sniffing like a dog. He smelled the poitín of course. He did a few "rounds" of the kitchen, and finally stopped in front of my father, slapped him on the back and shouted, "It's poitín, you devil, and I could murder a sup". Of course, he got a small drop and made "kitchen" out of it - made it last longer - then smacked his lips and said, "That poitín is the devil, 'twould warm the cockles of your heart".

Of course, poitín is still alive and well and can be lethal. If sipped in very tiny quantities, it can be fiery and pleasurable. But if slugged in long swigs, long and often, it can cause great harm, even death. So, if you happen to come on some poitín, sip it slowly and remember the old saying, "A drop of the craythur taken gently never hurt anybody".

Poitín was used at the corpse house, when a corpse was being waked. It was usually kept in the shed or the car house. The men were brought out and given a glass and were maith go leor or half merry after it. The women were never offered a glass of poitín, it was reserved for the more discriminating male palates. Sure if a woman was seen having a drop of poitín, there would be hell to pay and she'd never live it down. And anyhow, the men would say it would be a terrible shame to waste it on a woman. Bartley Mooney, Thomas Mooney's father, told my father once that he saw a man going to the wake three times and he got a sup of poitín each time. "Surely", said my father, "the man who was giving out the poitín saw him returning three times?" "Arra not at all", said Bartley, "sure he was so drunk, he didn't know who came because every time he gave a slug to somebody, he drank a slug himself".

As well as helping humans, poitín was often known to benefit the animals - calves in particular. I remember once the cow had a lovely white-headed calf. It was kind of frail for the first couple of hours and seemed unable to breathe, so my father decided it was time to introduce it to some poitín. Well, he gave it a small "steall" and the next thing, didn't the calf leap up and stagger round - front ways and sideways. It was as drunk as drunk could be! Suddenly, it circled round like a dog trying to catch its tail. It let back its head and emitted a loud "maaaa", before sighing deeply and healthily and lying down. The poor cow looked sideways at her offspring, lowed loudly as if to say in her bovine way - "Some mothers do have 'em". "Well", said my father, "did you ever see anything like that in all your born days! I declare to God, I could make a fortune raising half dead calves to life!"

So poitín played a large part in the life of the farmer and his family in my youth. It's still used today and I wonder how many men, sniffing its unusual aroma, could recognise it as Tom did so many years ago, and call out "It's poitín, you devil".

Kinvara as I first knew it

Reared as we were in a small rural isolated area, we viewed Kinvara town as a mecca and were drawn to it as to a magnet. We thought it was the be-all and end-all of everything. To spend an hour there was my greatest desire. I didn't want to have anywhere special to go - just to be there was enough.

My first visit to Kinvara was as a small child. A cousin on my father's side, Fr. Joseph Corless, was saying his first mass in the convent church and we all attended. My father couldn't go as he had to "mind the house" and milk the cows, feed the animals and generally stick around. But my mother took the four of us and we set off walking. Had I been going to America, I couldn't have been happier!

Two or three of the Hynes family - Peggy, Delia and Teresa - joined us, with the news that their mother had a new baby boy, Seán, the night before. In Nogra, Bridie and Frances Linnane came with us and I think Julia and Kathleen Carty. Off we marched the long, long road to Kinvara. The mass was uplifting and the choir was beautiful. We ran down to Mountain View Hotel and had minerals afterwards, before being marshalled together and shifted off home again. It was a short visit, but it was enough to whet the appetite.

However, I had to wait another year before my next visit, and that was another flying one. My younger sister, Julia, and I were sent for some message which was urgently needed. "Hurry on", we were told, "and if ye fall, don't wait to get up". We ran as far as Geata Bán, and didn't an archangel come in the form of Tommy Kavanagh on a man's bicycle. "I'll carry the two of ye", he said, "one on the carrier and one on the bar". We looked at him, then at each other and Julia hopped up on the carrier, legs stuck out so as to have no contact with the spokes, while I sat on the bar. It was most uncomfortrable but he huffed and puffed his way and dropped us outside the convent chapel – no doubt glad to be rid of us. We got the required message and set off again for home, but no matter how much we prayed, no cyclist appeared to give us a lift and only one car passed and it was going so slowly that we were quicker walking.

One year later, I was deemed old and responsible enough to be sent alone to Kinvara with a list of things to be done. "Be careful and mind what you have", warned my father. I wouldn't mind, but I had nothing, only about sixpence or so. "Leave in the rhubarb and fresh eggs to John Peter's", was first on the list. The smiling proprietor of Mountain View Hotel approached and immediately one felt enveloped by his welcome and his warmth. There was an appetising smell emanating from the kitchen, and I could hear somebody playing the piano in a front room. People came in and left non-stop - it was like a railway station with the comings and goings. Having concluded my business, I left and went in to Traynors. Mikey Traynor was a cobbler and the story was that, no matter how badly worn the footwear was, he could mend it. He sat at a kind of table with awls, hammers, nails, a last, tacks, and a sharp knife thrown around on it. Hanging up were some pieces of leather and some strands of hemp. The hemp was waxed and used to sew the leather. I had to collect a pair of my father's boots which had new toe-caps fitted. Soles, heels, taoibhins they could do it at home, but only the shoemaker could make a good job of toe-caps. The job cost one shilling. Bridgie, Mikey's sister, wrapped the boots in a newspaper. I fixed them on the carrier and once more I was on my way. My next stop was Katie and Chris Winkle's shop. It was beautifully kept and offered many kinds of sweets, biscuits and things in glassy-looking plastic bags. They also sold copies and pencils. My favourite sweets were the conversation lozenges – multi-coloured and flat, with a word or two written on each one - Bravo, Eat Me, Come On or Hello Love. I slipped one into my mouth and just loved to feel it melting and sliding down my throat. I was never too eager to share them, so I quickly ate them all up.

Down the street again, past Ellie Noone's shop. Many years before, it had been a very busy fish shop, but I only knew it as a kind of dark interior, with a big fat cat sleeping in the near empty window, on which a mirror hung with a sign which read - Guinness is good for you.

On then to Johnston's Hall, a very imposing building, the interior of which seemed to offer as many attractions as Aladdin's cave. It had been a shop at one stage and had large and wonderful bay windows for display purposes. Across the road, almost, was Connolly's forge, to which the farmers brought their horses to be shod, or their cart wheels to be mended. Then I remembered that I had to go into Hawse's, the tailor, and tell that my father said to be sure to have his báinín ready next week as the cold weather was around the corner. My father had always suffered from rheumatism and used to wear flannel underwear and a báinín during the winter, so he was making sure that everything would be ready. Hawse smiled when I delivered my message and said, "Sound as a bell", and I continued my down town trip. I passed a tiny shop where Ellie Ryan sold assorted sweets, all in rows of glass jars, some full and some half empty. Forde's shop was next and I left my bicycle against the wall while I looked through the window at all the gadgets nestling safely under the sparkling glass counter. I saw slides, rings, brooches and necklaces - all as far removed from me as if they were on Mars - with no money you can only look. Poor Peter Forde, with the gentle smile and soft voice, must have watched in despair as we stood outside, noses glued to the window, just looking, but longing for the day when we could jingle some coins, march in and buy as we wished.

My next call was to Mrs Flanagan's, the dress maker. I left my bicycle outside Flatley's pub and crossed the road. I had to collect a skirt for my sister, Mary, and while it was being wrapped, I had a good look at the clothes hanging up - some finished and some only half basted or

115

tacked. When I came out, I remember looking up at Winkle's Hotel in the square, opposite the weigh-house. It was well painted and well kept, with a row of cars parked outside. I longed for the day when I would be sent up for some message so I could get a closer look. Across the road was Corless's public house all lit up, another classy landmark. I walked down past Greene's pub, whom I knew were my cousins and on the corner was Annie Leech's shop where I bought Bull's Eyes and Peggy's Leg. A little further down, I feasted my eyes on the clothes in O'Halloran's windows, twin sets and flared jackets, before crossing the street and climbing the hill to the Post Office which was run by Mrs Mary Phelan, postmistress from 1922 to 1961. She was a gentle lady and I asked her was there any letter for Quinn's in Duras, as we had a postal service only every second day. She meticulously went through the pile of letters and on that particular day, my heart lifted when she handed me a letter addressed to my mother with an American date stamp, because I knew that such a letter nearly always contained some American dollars. I was in the Seventh Heaven.

Down the hill I freewheeled and into John Joe Shaughnessy's shop. I wanted a crossover for my mother and the minute I mentioned it, John Joe swung into action. He looked up her size in a book, danced over to a pile of crossovers, selected one, shook it out and when satisfied that it was alright, he refolded it and with a charming, charismatic smile asked, "Will there be anything else?" Then he wrapped it, wrote a docket, gave me my change and I was on my way to Helebert's. I looked across the road at Greene's, St. George's and Tyrells, but didn't dare visit when I hadn't been told. I bought a half quarter of common tobacco from Pat Helebert which cost about nine pence and went into Mattie Regan's for an Irish Press and was tongue tied when the boss himself asked me, "And how are all in Duras this weather?" Just imagine! He knew where I came from!

I looked longingly out the Castle Road, where a car disappeared and two cyclists pedalled and two or three people went for a walk. Where did it lead? At what age could I investigate the mysterious, for me, highway?

Would the day ever come when I could cycle out that road which led to the breathtaking unknown.

Then, laden down with my messages, I headed for home and resolved that in a very short time, Kinvara would be revisited.

For better or for worse

Matchmaking was a fact of life in Ireland about the turn of the century. In Duras, it was no exception, a means used to get a man a wife or get a woman a husband. Sometimes the negotiations took place in a pub where pints and mediums, or half pints, kept things and people well oiled. Sometimes meetings took place in the home; again things were helped on the way by tea and poitín. It was usually the man who travelled - either to the pub or to a house. A friend nearly always accompanied him - to sing his praises and advise him. The father, uncle or brother spoke up for the girl. A dowry or fortune was given to the girl but, to be honest, it wasn't much, as the people were very poor. Very often, if the eldest child was a daughter who grew up to be a plainlooking girl whom nobody wished to marry, she'd have to accept any offer for her hand, move out and leave space for her brother to get married and bring in a wife. Mostly the girls passively accepted whatever plans were made and went along with whatever directives were given. Some matches were made and the pair concerned never even saw each other until the morning of the wedding.

Often much conniving went on when strangers from a couple of parishes away came to look for a husband for some woman and look over the place for her. The whole village banded together in loyalty and tried to pull the wool over the visitor's eyes. The farmer in question would borrow two or three cows and maybe a horse from the neighbours and put them in to the fields around the house. Having a good number of animals on display in this way would prove that he was a well to do man, and that any woman in her right senses would be only too happy to be buried with his people. But, if the locals were cute and devious, so were the visitors. A word or two of advice was always handed to them before they left their own homes - "Siúl thart agus coinnigh súil ar an gcarn aoiligh". This means that they should walk around outside the man's house and in particular, keep an eye on the dung hill or the dung heap. And sound advice it was too, because if the dung hill was fairly big, then the animals were permanent and belonged to the farmer, but if the dung hill was small, then the animals had been borrowed and the visitors departed without making any deal. "I don't know in the name of God why they weren't satisfied", said one such farmer, "especially as I had so many animals on show for them!" "Well, do you know", said his neighbour, "I think that you frightened them away. They thought you were too much of a big shot. You had a right to tell them that you were one man, one horse, one pig. If you don't tell the truth, you'll end up one man without a woman".

Several other stories about matchmaking spring to mind and I'll start by mentioning that my own parents' marriage was a match. My mother, Julia Folan from Knock, Spiddal, had emigrated to America when she was about seventeen years of age. She went to Boston where it was a home away from home as she had five brothers and two sisters there with her. She came back to Ireland on a holiday after several years and was spotted by my father as she went to Mass. Incidentally, my father was on holidays at his eldest sister's home - Faherty's pub in Knock. My father bombarded everybody with questions about her when suddenly the lady in question walked into the shop. Contact was made and a match negotiated. They were married and spent the honeymoon in O'Leary's Hotel in Salthill. Two days they stayed. On the second day, my father decided he'd go to the bar for a couple of pints and my mother decided she'd go for a short walk down the street. After three pints, my father went outside and saw this smashing lady with luxuriant brown hair piled high on her head and dressed in a navy suit, coming towards him. "Hello", she said, smiling at him. "Hello", he said, "I'm waiting for my wife". "I'm your wife", she said.

"Well, begod if you are", he said, "It suits me fine, and if I'm having a dream, I don't want to wake up". She looked so lovely he couldn't believe his luck. Next day they went back to Duras in a side car driven by Jack Greene.

The driver was stopped by the gardaí. They were travelling by sidecar and my father used to get great satisfaction talking about how "they foxed the cops". It seems that they had a large bottle of poitin for the homecoming hooley. Out of the blue appeared two gardaí signalling "stop" to the driver. It was twilight, and the sidecar was pulled in to the side of the road. Quick thinkingly, my father jumped down on the grassy bank and threw the bottle into the roadside bushes. Meanwhile, the gardaí did a quick search and, finding nothing, cycled away. My father waited until they disappeared around the corner and then he retrieved the precious bottle from the briars and nettles, hopped up in the sidecar and away trotted the horse to Duras, where the bottle of poitin met a very sudden death. Years later, when my father told the story to the gardaí, they said, "Sure we knew well - but we'd never rob you on your honeymoon". "I don't believe that", said my father, "I believe ye'd rob ye'er own mothers, if ye got the chance".

Some funny things happened while matches were being negotiated. Once Tom and his father, from Clarinbridge, went to Hanrahan's Pub in Gort to meet John and his daughter. John and his daughter came from outside Gort. Both parties had travelled by horse and cart and met inside in the snug. When Tom's father took one look at the young woman who was very common and plain and actually smoked a pipe, he turned to his son and said one word, "Tackle". Of course, he meant "Go and tackle the horse and we'll go home - I don't think much of her". But poor Tom misread or misunderstood and he made one grab at the girl and "tackled" her, put his arms round her and tried to kiss her. Her father yelled blue murder and that put an end to that. No match resulted, but had they been left alone without parental interference, who knows but they'd have had a good marriage. Maybe she had enjoyed being "tackled"!

Some men were hoodwinked and codded whilst matchmaking. An incident happened when Pat went looking for a wife. He thought he was getting a very attractive young woman, but when he turned around at the altar, he almost collapsed when he saw another daughter, not a patch on her sister. His best man, also his brother, whispered, "Smash the match" - but he didn't. He kept his cool, married the girl and they had a great marriage and a marvellous family.

Although most girls were submissive and did exactly as they were told, some rebelled and left. One such lady was Sabina Cloonan from Caherfourvase, Craughwell. She was a very beautiful young woman of nineteen years and her father came home from the fair one day with an old man in tow. He was surely sixty years - féasógach, and whiskery, bandy-legged, thin, staggery and rheumaticky. Added to that was the fact that he wore big black wellingtons and a raggedy shirt. But he had land, lots of land. Sabina took one look at him and instantly decided, "I'll never marry him - never. Sure he wouldn't even make a middlin' scarecrow". So she left and went off to Australia. Her adventures I'll leave for another day - suffice it to say that her grandchildren live in the magnificent Blue Mountains outside Sydney today - where would they be living if she had married "grandad"?

The wedding feast was usually held the night before - dancing, singing, eating and drinking. There was a lot of food - three or four roasted geese, bacon and cabbage. The bacon was American at four pence a pound. Lots of brown bread and currant cakes were baked. An odd loaf could be bought. Bottles of poitín, hidden outside, were brought in and the feasting continued all night. Once a man got cold feet when he saw all the food his future wife was devouring. He crept out and saddled up his horse and belted off home. But he hadn't gone far, when her three brothers caught up with him and brought him back - he was drunk next morning, but very soon settled down as he discovered that if she could eat, his wife could certainly earn and was a great help to him.

Great attention was given to a new woman when she came to live in a village. The first Sunday at Mass must have been a nightmare. She set off for the church by herself - it would take a JCB to make a husband go with her. She was minutely inspected by all the "nosey parkers". All of her faults were commented on, while her good qualities went unnoticed. She was either too tall, or too small, too thin or too fat. She was either too talkative or too quiet. If she was a happy type of person who laughed easily - "Isn't she flighty and a bit airy-fairy". If she was a quiet girl who kept her mind to herself - "Isn't she snooty, and I wouldn't mind only where she came from". So it was a very slow process to become one of the villagers, burrow into the local community, make her own niche and be accepted.

Where were the women?

This has been a vexed question for many years - this and a few others. What did the women do? Men were both seen and heard. Why were women seldom seen and never heard?

Actually, when I was growing up - men took central stage and women were quite happy, or seemed to be quite happy, to remain in the background. The men made the important decisions and the women abided by them. Really, the men were the bosses everywhere - on the farm and in the home. The women acted out the roles of servility, while the men were in authority. Some women were heads of their own kitchens, but could do very little without the husband's permission.

Expectations for women of my mother's generation were not very high, but they improved as the century progressed. Women were expected to be good cooks and good money managers. They were expected to make sixpence stretch as far as a shilling. They must be able to sew and knit. They must be able to cope in a crisis - able to sit up all night watching a sick child and still arise, bright-eyed and bushy tailed at cock shout next morning. They must have had marvellous stamina and wonderful courage. Some of them lived in remote, lonely, isolated places and had to face all kinds of illnesses and tough times all alone, but they did it and, more often than not, emerged triumphant.

The women cooked and baked, knitted and sewed, scrubbed and shone - and listened. Some of the men were complainers and moaners - wives listened. Some of the husbands were rude and unapproachable - wives listened. Some of the men were selfish and self centred - wives listened. Some of the men were dogmatic and dictatorial - wives listened. Some of the men were cruel and heartless - wives listened. Some of the men loved themselves and only existed for themselves - wives meekly existed, almost apologetically. This meek role was the one dictated by the system, by society and by the menfolk. And as we approach the end of the second millenium, I am very pleased to see that it's a role of the past. With our lady President exhorting Mna na hEireann to stand up and be counted, it is my earnest wish that never again will women be expected to lead the kind of lives they led at the turn of the century.

One lady, whom I knew very well when I was a child, was a marvellous worker, a great cook and a wonderful wife and mother. Her days were spent working not only in the house, but also on the farm. Her husband was the greatest good-for-nothing I've ever met. And they made a great team because, from the beginning, she made it clear that she was quite prepared to work like a man, provided there was no interference from Johnny, who, in all truth, was a bit of a "dudan", or slow witted. He was slow and couldn't be trusted to do anything properly. Indeed, he couldn't be trusted to do anything at all. So Johnny decided, "anything for a quiet life", and his wife ran the show, and did it very well too and they prospered. I often wondered why more women didn't do as she did, and reverse the roles.

In most homes, women were overworked and undernourished and underconsidered. Expecting a baby nowadays straight away puts a woman on a kind of pedestal, to be pampered and shown excessive consideration, to be spoiled and babied. In the old days, being pregnant or, as they said then, in the family way, was just another chore to be got through with the least amount of expense and the minimum trouble or disruption. The expectant mother did all the usual jobs as well as going into the fields to help with the farmwork. No extra consideration was expected and none given. As there were no methods of birth control, there was no limit to the number of children in any one family. But some fathers did discipline themselves and some just didn't. There was one lady I knew who had twelve children and later was grandmother to fortyeight grandchildren. "Wasn't twelve children a lot to have?", I questioned her once. "Musha, it was", she said, "and too many. But the winters were cold and we used to go to bed early . . ."! The majority of men demanded that the women stay at home and bake, cook, wash, iron and clean. They should have babies and rear them, not voicing any opinions, not gallivanting and not demanding anything. This was the role designed by men for their women folk, though not all the men, I must add. This was the part they had to play in the drama of life, the roles of reproduction and servility.

Nowadays, fathers take a very active and interested role in the rearing of their children. They can change nappies, feed with bottles, take for walks and generally replace the mother when the need arises. Not so when I was growing up. The wife bore the children and she reared them as well. I met a woman who told me that she hadn't been to Kinvara for five years. In that length of time, she had given birth to four children, as well as working on the farm and running the house. She didn't seem to think that she had missed anything. "Musha", she said, "what on earth would I want in Kinvara? Himself does all the messages and gets all the commands while I keep the home fires burning", as indeed she did and very efficiently too. And she was only one of many. She was representative of wives of that era, who expected little and got even less.

"And why do you put up with it?", I asked one poor woman, who had just told me that her husband viewed all women as second class citizens and her, in particular, as an unpaid slave. She polished his shoes, laid his Sunday clothes on the back of the chair before the fire to take off the chill, had his breakfast "ready on the dot", and his every wish was her command. She made excuses when he drank a pint too many and she hid in the shed when he was "on the warpath". "I put up with it", she said, "'cos I'd do anything for a quiet life. And I'm just biding my time until my two sons grow up. Then we'll teach him a lesson". And they did too, when one day he overstepped himself and hit her. Boy, oh boy, it was the first and only wallop.

125

NOT A WORD OF A LIE

Thinking of some women's pained faces, I often wonder how did they put up with the authoritative, dictatorial, rude and cynical menfolk. And the women daren't confide in anybody. There was no such thing as an agony aunt or a Woman's Way columnist. There was nobody who could say, "Well, what are your options?" There were no options - only stick it out. Usually things righted themselves, but the odd one just endured. Many women simply had to endure their lot. They had no choice.

Some people nowadays may think that long ago the worst thing that could happen to a girl was that she be married to a puny self-centred specimen. But in my estimation, an unmarried woman keeping house for a brother or for a set of brothers or even for an in-law, was abused even more. It was slave labour. It was inhuman bondage. It was committment without ties. It was life without living. You owned nothing, in spite of giving years of your life, slaving and labouring. And your expectations were nil, because the minute an in-law came in, out went the spinster aunt, faster than you'd say "go". And nobody cared. And these women lived and died, working in the homes of somebody else for nothing, not even a sure seat on the hob. They had no legal status, and were without protection of any kind. Life consisted of work, work and then - more work.

I've been toying with the idea of writing about one special hardworking, kind, neighbourly, agreeable, woman, but I honestly could not pick out just one. I can remember dozens of them - Molly Sullivan, Maggie Hynes, Mary Farrell, Nonie Fahy, Delia Carty, Susan Connors, Nora Whelan, Agnes Connors, Sarah Hynes, Mary Jane Shaughnessy, Mary Tereasa Linnane, Ellen McCook, Kate Forde, Nora Jordan, Sarah Moloney, Lena Connors - they were the salt of the earth, and each one in her own way merits writing about. All of them lived noble, hardworking lives, reared families, and made "ends meet". Each life deserves a chapter and no chapter, however long or meticulously written, could contain descriptions of all they went through.

My own mother, Julia, was a rare specimen of womanhood. She had travelled a lot in America before she settled down in Duras. Surely the transition must have been difficult. She must have missed the cities, shops, mansions. She must have hankered after the clean life in Boston, San Francisco, Los Angeles or Chicago. All of the places, which to us were names, to her were real and had been home to her for a year at a time. But being young and flighty, we didn't really listen to her as she told us of her travels. She had witnessed an earthquake in Monterey. She had visited Washington, with five feet of snow on the ground. She had travelled from Boston to Arizona by Pullman train which pulled in every night and the blinds were drawn as the passengers slept. She had visited Niagara Falls and saw a man throw himself over. As I said, I could write a book alone about her. But back she came and settled down in Duras and must have found the life extremely constricting and restraining, insipid and unexciting. She had funds of stories to tell and one of the nicest memories I have of the long winter's nights, rare, but they did occur when nobody came to cuairt, was when, to while away an hour, my mother would start, "I remember". She told us once that she was a competitor in a quiz show in New York and stood to win a hundred dollars, which probably would have changed her whole life had she won it. The six mark question was "Which should you do, eat to live or live to eat?" She answered, "Eat to live", when the quizmaster with a triumphant smile and a loud yahoo announced, "Wrong - we should live to eat". So she didn't win, and maybe it was just as well, or otherwise I mightn't be here now.

And what about the "hidden" women all over Ireland? Where were they? Some of them were stagnating in laundries, homes and "head-case" institutions. These "hidden" women were the ones who had blotted their lily-white, virginal copy-books. They were the unfortunates who had babies before tying the all-important knot of marriage. They were called the penitent women, and nobody wanted to know them, help them or even be seen to be friendly with them. They had nowhere to go. The system of the time ordained that these women should be put away, should be barred from contaminating others, should be incarcerated forever, should be confined for life to a nightmare. For one sin, one slippage, one mistake, they were plucked out of society and banished by fathers, mothers, brothers or sisters. Thereafter, until death, the poor unfortunate, untimely mothers spent their miserable lives, washing and ironing in the laundries, or cooking, scrubbing and cleaning in some kind of home, with none of the love or warmth of a proper home.

And it became a kind of vicious circle. A young girl became pregnant and to avoid the disgrace and stigma, the poor victim was carted off by her family to a safe spot, where she would never be seen or heard of again. As soon as the door closed behind her, so did her place in the family circle end, so did her name cease to be spoken, so did she literally disappear off the face of the earth.

Let's go behind the closed doors and follow the story of one such poor young woman for a while. She worked and slaved while waiting for the baby to come - washed and scrubbed and ironed - day in, day out, paying lip service to prayers, acting like a zombie. Then her baby came into this harsh, cruel world and another link in the chain of bondage was forged. The baby was usually left in the mother's care until it was nine weeks old, and then it was wrenched from her enveloping arms and put into an orphanage. The bereft mother was of course distraught and, to be honest, some were never quite sane again. They missed their babies and some even carried around paper-babies or raggy-dolls, on which they lavished all their love and to which they spoke in baby-talk. There was no hope of liberation except by death or by escaping. Occasionally, I have heard that some tried to escape, but were hauled back and this was a sure tell-tale giveaway to the outside world, had the world been listening. They must have longed for family, friends, home. They must have had hopes and dreams which were destined never to be fulfilled. Their hearts must have been literally broken at this enforced entombment. But that was how society dictated, and that was the appeasement demanded. Years passed while the mother worked and grew older, and her baby grew up in the orphanage and, in time, if not placed for adoption, it was often recruited into the ranks of the laundry-workers, in turn to scrub and wash and clean, until death brought release.

One may wonder why wasn't help forthcoming from those in charge of the institutions. Well, they were only doing their jobs and it is not fair to allocate blame. If any blame was to be apportioned, it was to the family of the banished women. Meanwhile, the women responsible for the smooth running of the institutions were nuns, novices, postulants and nurses. They did their level best to help the women, but God knows they had their own troubles. They had vows to keep, prayers to say, bills to pay, work to do and little time to spend with their charges. They couldn't allow a woman to leave, if her family didn't ask for her. They couldn't place a woman in another employment if her family didn't approve and very often, indeed almost always, the family didn't want to know about, hear about or ask about the poor woman once she was taken off their hands. So the blame must be laid squarely on the heads of the people who sent away the poor woman, the immediate families. May God forgive them. But again, society and the system had laid down the rules, and the poor, at least, must abide by them. It annoys me to think that the poor women had to suffer so much, while the men, responsible for their condition, got off scot free. The women were removed, while the men were left alone, free to perpetrate more crimes and cause other women to be sent away.

But, thank God, progress has been made and major steps taken to allow women to live their chosen lifestyles and never again, in this country anyhow, will women have to play second fiddle to men. Never again will women be used by men as playthings and then cast aside. Never again will women be put away for doing something which they couldn't possible have done alone. Long live Mná na hÉireann.

The Piebald Ass

Nowadays, asses are a "scarce" animal - very rarely seen and very rarely heard. In Duras of long ago, the majority of farmers owned an ass or two each, so it was no great "gaisce" or feat to see an ass in every second field. They were used to carry light loads, to carry light men and to pull light carts.

The moment we heard an ass braying his loud, coarse, throaty "he-haw", we always thought of death. The old supersitition was that every time an ass brayed, it was a signal that somebody had died suddenly, and the somebody was almost always a traveller. To this day, I know one old man who "kinda" still believes it. I was in my teens before an elderly neighbour, Pat Sullivan, pityingly informed me that it was all a yarn - "Musha, God help you, a girleen", he said, "he's braying because he is getting frisky; how in the name of God would that stupid ass know of a death, when he doesn't even know to get out of his own way".

My father owned an ass which two or three of us girls almost killed. The poor old ass was grazing happily in the field when one of us issued a dare. The challenge was to catch the animal and ride him around the paddock. But we didn't reckon on how "dána" the asal could be. We ran after him, before him, around him. We "flocked" him in a corner, but "he got away on us". He ran, raced and galloped. He kicked up his hind legs, up and out, and did his best to injure us. We ran him ragged and indeed ran ourselves ragged as well. If the poor ass was out of breath, then so were we. We were scarcely able to run, but were determined to wear him down, more especially as we had noticed a slight slackening in his speed, and a slight loss of height in his kick. Things were looking good when our sport was interrupted by an almighty screech from my father. He was standing on the haggard wall like a "standpike". He looked like the Statue of Liberty with a camóg in one hand which was raised threateningly. The fist of the other hand was being shaken menacingly in our direction. "Leave that ass alone", he roared, "or I'll malafouster ye". It had the desired effect, because we scattered all sides and away ran the ass, bucking and lepping off up the paddock. To add insult to injury and to make matters worse, the ass brayed long and loud - as if to say "I'll live to bray another day". As indeed he did, and he actually lived to be a very old grey ass who, with the familiarity of longevity, was allowed the freedom of the haggard. Once he munched the top of a young tree, sown only the previous week, at which criminal action my father was heard to remark, "Musha, it wouldn't feed a dreoilín all he ate, and anyhow it wasn't a great tree" - excuses for an old friend.

Jack Whelan owned an ass and one morning when he went out to tackle him, he found him dead. Jack didn't mention the word "dead", rather he said, "The craythur was stretched and not a stir out of him". So he decided to go to the next fair in Kinvara to buy another ass, "Otherwise", he said, "I'll have to do the ass's jobs myself and to tell the truth, I'd prefer to have an ass to do them". At the fair he saw a fine, lively piebald ass - black with white patches, owned by a traveller, who was accompanied by half a dozen snotty-nosed youngsters. Jack saw other asses, but he kept coming back to this one, again and again. He liked a wiry all black ass being sold near Mattie Regan's shop. He liked a stocky grey ass tethered to a cart opposite the courthouse. But he really fell for the piebald ass being walked around the square. Several times, he circled him and more than the strong legs, more than the alert head, he liked the piebald look. "God knows", he thought to himself, "many farmers in Duras have asses, but not one has a piebald ass - so for this reason, I'll buy Neddy, the patchy piebald". So he spent an hour making a bargain, and finally left the fair the proud possessor of this unique animal. He cycled home, holding the rope attached to the ass, whistling with pride. Next day, he "tried out" the ass who did everything "báways" - he stayed going when told to stop, he stopped when told "g'wan", he backed when urged forward and when the notion took him, he stuck his back legs in to the ground and refused to budge.

"Well", said Jack, when telling me the story years later, "did you ever hear 'chomh dána le asal? That's exactly what the piebald was - the boldest ass I have ever seen. But", continued Jack, "that wasn't the end of the story at all, at all. After a couple of days, didn't I notice that the white patches weren't as white as they were in the beginning and my piebald ass was fast turning into a black ass. The whole truth dawned the day the ass scratched himself on the gate, and some of the very dry paint flaked off. I knew then what an amhlóir or fool I had been. The travellers had sold me a "painted piebald". So Jack plotted and planned and bided his time and worked the, by now, black ass, and all the time his fertile brain was working at top speed. And one day, about six months later, his patience was rewarded. didn't he see the travellers camped near Moy Cross, the same crowd that had tried to sell him the "dud". And what was grazing on the side of the road but a lovely young piebald ass - a real one this time. Jack did his business in Kinvara and cycled home as if all the síoga in the country were after him. He enlisted the aid of his nephew, Mattie Quinn, swore him to silence and if the proposed "exchange" was successful, he promised him a day at the races in Galway. Bhí go maith is ní raibh go holc. That night they went into action. They put a súgán or straw rope on the ass's hooves to eliminate noise and tied an old scarf around his mouth to deter him from braying and thus announcing his presence to the whole world. They walked him smartly as far as Moy road. The whole encampment was in complete darkness except for the light of the moon. Silence reigned over all as it's a very well known fact that travellers go to bed early and rise with the crack of dawn. The piebald ass was lying down a little way from the tents. Jack crept in quietly, reached the ass, tied a scarf around his mouth and led him quietly along the grassy bank and made for home. He didn't trot him on the road for a quarter of a mile at least, in case his hooves re-echoed in the quiet of the night. You may wonder where the nephew was all this time? He was waiting patiently on the side of the road, accompanied by the 'piebald' and he remained there for twenty minutes. When he thought Jack was half way home, he led the ass on to the spot where the real piebald had been lying. He removed the socks and the scarf and scampered off like a "scalded cat". Not a dog barked. Not an ass brayed. Not one word was spoken while the "swap" took place. Jack and his nephew reached home in "high glee!" and straight away proceeded to give the ass a bit of a face-lift. They cut off his tail, at least half of it. They plaited and braided his mane. Then they put a "brand" on his leg - a patch of tar - and then awaited results. Next day, at about one o'clock, the travellers arrived - two men and a young boy. Jack stood on the pillar of the gate and counted them as the pony and cart came over the hill and straight away sent his nephew for his neighbour, Sonny Kavanagh, "extra reinforcements", he said, "in case of trouble". He was afraid that he would need brawn as well as brain. The conversation between Jack and the traveller went as follows:

Traveller: I see you have a piebald ass there.

Jack: Well, if you see that, it's a good sign you aren't blind.

Traveller: But that's my ass, sir. You pinched him.

Jack: Wrong, a mac. It was your ass, but I bought him from you in Kinvara at the October fair – don't you remember me? I'm the eejit who bought your piebald ass.

Traveller: I say you stole him last night, sir.

Jack: Don't be danach (daft) man. I bought him from you and all my neighbours know it – and God knows, it was a great day's work.

Traveller: But it wasn't a piebald ass I sold you last October, sir.

Jack: Oh, now you're talking, man. It certainly wasn't a piebald ass you sold me, and if the gárdái catch you for selling me a "painted" ass, you'll be brought to court, and maybe rot in jail for many a long year. By the way, here comes my neighbour, and by the same token, he's a guard.

Traveller: I'm going now, but I'll be back......

Jack: Not if you're wise, you won't. Paint the "dud" and

sell him again, but don't ever be seen around here again or . . .

And he never did return, and Jack always said, when telling the story years later, "It was the best swap ever made and the best night's work ever done".

People were totally opposed to beating an ass with any kind of whip or stick. Because the poor creature had "carried Mary and Jesus to safety", it has since been considered a sacred animal. Old people always said that across its back ran the sign of the cross, but I must admit that I never investigated this too closely, so I cannot vouch for its veracity.

Included in the ass family was the jennet - a cross between an ass and a pony. It was a big ugly animal with a square head, long ears and prancing feet. I remember watching two boys fighting in the school playground when I was in sixth class. One fellow looked at the other and said "You look just like a jennet", and all hell broke loose. Evidently the jennet was not a popular look-a-alike!

Some farmers kept mules, the product of a female horse and a male donkey, but again they were scarce enough. Once I heard my father saying that "a neighbour was taken to hospital last night having been kicked by a mule". Months later, when I enquired how the patient was, I was told that he was "just beginning to come alive, as the kick from the mule shook the living daylights out of him and he didn't know day from night". Ever afterwards, I can tell you, I steered clear of a mule, just in case his high kicking hind legs gravitated towards me.

Much lore was attached to the ass or the donkey. When somebody had light fingers and helped himself to things which did not belong to him, it was said about him that "he'd whip the cross off an ass's back". When children were annoying or teasing an older person, to frighten them off he'd say, "If I catch you, I'll put an ass's head on you" - signal for exodus straight away. Once, I heard a farmer giving instructions to his dog, directions which, however, the dog never obeyed. And the farmer, in frustration, shouted "You are as stupid as an ass, only not half as useful".

Even such a lowly and servile creature as the ass could, and did, prompt poems and stories to be written about him. One of the best known stories about an ass is "M'Asal Beag Dubh" by Páraic O'Conaire, part of which is actually set in Kinvara.

And I hasten to add that the tale of the piebald ass was told and retold and passed many a long winter's night pleasantly and humorously around the blazing fires in Duras long ago.

On-going struggles

I reland has a long history of struggling, often against the odds, but never, or rarely, admitting defeat. It was much as it had always been in the little community of Duras during the "Thirties" and "Forties".

It was a struggle just to stay alive. T.B. was rampant and seemed to look to the poorer in society to satisfy its voracious appetite. It snatched its victims at any age and, indeed, it cruelly destroyed whole families at one stroke. The nearest doctor was in Kinvara, but very often he was not sent for until the disease had reached an advanced stage, and by then he was too late to administer help. Babies, especially, had a very high mortality rate and there are many babies buried in the old graveyard in Parkmore - laid low by the scythe of disease.

This struggle to survive against ill-health and disease was very, very harrowing, especially as it was against an unknown quantity, a mysterious and implacable enemy, a deadly killer who had no compunction in exacting his pound of flesh. Once I heard my father saying, "You'd have some satisfaction when you could punch the enemy in the nose". But with sickness, there's nothing or nobody to punch.

It was a continuous struggle to make ends meet down on the farms. Indeed, the farms were only "holdings" of ten or twenty acres each and not all good land. The farmers struggled all day, every day, from morning till night in all kinds of weather. They braved the worst elements to pick potatoes, cut seaweed, pull and crown beet, plough and harrow rock hard land. They sowed and reaped and just barely kept "a bite in their mouths". And there was the eternal ongoing struggle against the

136

elements. As John Glynn used to say, "The rain holds off for nobody".

I remember once my father had a fine field of barley ready to reap, as fine and as healthy as you'd wish to see. There wasn't even one rib of baráiste left growing in it and there were two scarecrows in each headland in case the crows were tempted to sample it. My father sent word to the meitheal - Mattie Quinn, Mickey Keane, Mick Linnane, Thomas Mooney - and ordered them, yes, ordered them, to come next morning early, "to see, in the name of God, if we'd manage to knock the field of barley before the weather breaks". Alas!, that night the weather broke. The rain fell in sheets and a storm blew. Next morning the barley was flattened or "lodged", as they called it, and all of the grain was lost. I can still, in my mind's eye, see my father deep in thought as he surveyed the scene, while the hens committed gluttony and ate every thing in sight. No doubt he was wondering how would he now pay the bills which should have been paid by the barley money.

I can tell you that things were tight for a while in the struggle to feed and clothe the family. But a lesson was obviously learned, because about two years later, Tommy Kilkelly sowed wheat in a field next to our house. It grew into a marvellous crop of lovely yellow corn rippling in the gently whispering wind. Tommy always used the hook, an corrán, to cut the corn, a very slow and backbreaking job. Anyhow, my father came home from work that evening, untackled and fed the horse, all the time scanning the sky. He went in to eat his dinner and was out again in a few minutes, again looking at the sea and the sky. He called one of us and said urgently, "Cycle to Tommy Mhicil's, and tell him to come down and we'll start cutting right away. Tomorrow will be too late, and call Sonny Sullivan on your way up". He sent somebody else for Martin Hynes and down bóithrín hAinlí for Thomas Mooney. John Glynn and Patrick Connors and Jack Moloney were cutting for themselves and couldn't come. It was still bright when they invaded the cornfield and the scythes were soon swishing murderously through the precious wheat, laying it low from headland to headland. In the meantime, Tommy arrived and his heart must have done a somersault when he saw the crowd swarming all over his field, though he knew it was for his own good. So they cut, and bound and stooked. And just as well they did, because at 7.00 am next morning, the heavens opened, the rain poured down in torrents and the wind wickedly gusted in whirwinds. Not an ear of corn would have been saved.

The following Sunday, when Tommy came to thank my father, he questioned him, "And how were you so sure the weather wouldn't hold?" "Well", said my father, "two years ago, I didn't read the weather signs properly, or let's say, I read them but didn't heed them, so I lost all of the barley, but this time I read them and heeded them. Once bitten, twice shy".

So year after year, the farmers and the elements locked in an ongoing battle, each side winning some and losing some. Where there were large families, they always seemed to be hungry, with insatiable appetites. Mothers were worn and thin and badly nourished. Fathers were "old before their time" and many died prematurely from overwork, malnutrition and, sometimes, even a neglected cold. But those humble and hungry beginnings didn't deter the boys and girls - or at least the majority of them - from growing up and moving on. Perhaps it was because of, rather that in spite of, their struggling beginnings that all the youngsters of that time had an innate desire to survive, at all costs.

There were intense struggles to keep the bills paid. There was no such thing as a steady income, rather a few pounds came in fits and starts and sometimes not at all. What came did so irregularly from various sources. We got advance beet cheques. We got ordinary beet cheques. We got money which came from the sale of barley, cattle, sheep, calves or even pigs. We got paid for lorries of seaweed, bags of carrageen moss, and the odd dozen eggs. We got some money from the sale of wheat, or oats. Carts of potatoes and turnips were sold and after the sheep being shorn, we had fleeces of wool. And, of course, the odd cheque arrived from America to save the family from the perpetual struggle of having to make ends meet and count every penny.

The struggle for education was very much in evidence

in my young days. According to most men, you didn't need to spend anytime in a secondary school in order to be able to run a small farm. Why then, they asked, waste time and money learning English literature or French when there would never be an opportunity to use them. But to break out of that mould, designed for us, was an intense struggle and a big effort. My mother, having travelled, knew the value of and necessity for it and used to say, "Education is no load". And she must have spent hours talking to and at my father until he finally agreed that his four lovely lassies should be educated. I don't think that we ever thanked them sufficiently. My mother, with great foresight, used to walk the three miles to Seamount College every Sunday to teach Irish conversation to the boarders so that, when our turn came to attend the College, the fees were reduced considerably out of consideration for the brilliant work which my mother had done. What a struggle it must have been, when all around at the time it was deemed silly, a waste of time and totally out of character that girls should be educated.

But having got to secondary school, it was an entirely new struggle to stay there and do our best to contend with all the new areas into which we were catapulted. We had to compete with the "rich girls" from Galway and Dublin or Sligo who boarded there. We had to brave the long exhausting journey twice a day - about six miles. Our bicycles were secondhand, bacadaigh, with bald tyres, dodgy brakes, peeling saddle covers and warped wheels. We pedalled to and from, did our chores every evening and did our homework every night, all the time aided and abetted by our mother. She undertook some of our jobs so we could have more time to study. She got up very early some mornings to iron a blouse which had been washed the night before. She, it was, who rejoiced with us when we did well, and who sympathized with us when we did badly, but always admonished us, "You cannot be a winner always but don't ever stay down, get up and try again". She it was who had the huge kitchen fire blazing and the parlour fire lit when we came in on winter evenings, dripping wet, cold, hungry, tired and famished. And the struggles continued, my mother and father struggling to give us a good education, we struggling to be responsive and soak up everything like blotting paper, and other elements struggling to deter us and prevent us from scaling our "Everests". And, finally, there was the struggle to break out of the tight, limited, constricting mould, cast by the community and by local culture, into which we were supposed to fit. At a very early age, I scrutinised the role which I was supposed to play and decided it wasn't for me. At the earliest opportunity, I would abandon it. Geata Bán was for me the gateway to a new world and I couldn't wait to get out. I struggled against customs, culture, local traditions and the expectations of others and knew I would end up by hurting people. But I also knew I would make the effort and struggle hard to make my own life as successful as possible.

And the struggling didn't end there. It continued and still continues as I struggle to get my book published, to stay healthy, to keep the wrinkles at bay, to enjoy life to the full as I know that this life is not a dress-rehearsal, but the real thing.

Kitchens - old and new

Recently I stood in my own modern kitchen, with all its appliances and drawers full of gadgets and I couldn't help remembering my mother's kitchen. Nothing modern there. No appliances. No gadgets. And I must confess that the work done in that kitchen of long ago was just as efficient, the cooking just as delicious and the meals just as punctual as they are in my kitchen. Granted, more work was involved long ago - indeed, much more work.

Let me name the differences first and later I'll consider them at length. No running water. No electric cooker. No washing machine. No electric iron. No toaster. No electric kettle. No fridge. No bathroom.

Nowadays, running water is at our finger tips. We walk to the sink, turn on the tap and whoosh, water spills into the sink. Now consider the water problems in Duras in my young days. My own family was lucky because my father built a tank off the shed. It still stands and is still used. Fed by the eaveshoots and straight rain, it collected water very quickly. Every autumn it was allowed to run dry, was cleaned out and then whitewashed inside and was all set for the winter rains. There was a tap which was covered every frosty night with a sack to prevent it being frozen. This water was used for washing, cooking and feeding animals.

Other families who had no tanks, collected water in barrels left under the eaveshoots. If it rained, they had water. If it didn't, they walked to the well and carried home two buckets of water - one in each hand. I remember a lady, Mrs Jane Forde, who lived in Kinturla. She used to twist a scarf or small shawl in a special way like a turban. This she put on the crown of her head and lifted the bucket full of water on it. Away she walked, swinging her arms, carrying the bucket on her head with the grace and dignity of a queen wearing a crown.

Still other families, especially those who lived in Geeha and Aughinish, had to set three or four barrels on a horse cart and drive the six miles to the well. They filled up the barrels with water by carrying the buckets up and down the steps - steep and dangerous. Then they drove home over bad roads, and half of the water could splash out of the barrels. So, when they finally reached home, the barrel might be only half full and the water was therefore used sparingly and often was recycled. The journey could take them three or four to five hours. Just imagine wanting a cup of tea, finding the barrel empty and the nearest well six miles away. Was that difficult? Was that drudgery? And the worst feature was, there was no solution to the problem.

Let me say a word or two about Tobar Pháraic or The Well. Once, folklore says, there was a shortage of water in Duras. St. Patrick, who was preaching in the Burren, heard about it, came and had compassion. He stuck his crozier into the ground and fresh water gushed forth from the spot. In Irish, it reads thus: "Thosaigh Naomh Páraic ag guidhe agus taréis bomaite sháigh sé a bhacall sa talamh. As an bpoll beag sin, leím struth fíoruisce agus bhí áthas ar chuile dhuine". (St. Patrick prayed and after a moment, he stuck his crozier in the ground. From that small hole, a stream of fresh water flowed and everyone was happy). Of course folklore also tells us that the pagan chieftain of the area was displeased and he laid a curse or incantation on the well. But St. Patrick parried it and said, "Má thiteann an mallacht go mba ar adharc na mbó a thitfidh sé". Translated that means, "If the curse falls, may it fall on the cow's horns." So, as a result, the people of Duras have always enjoyed fresh water from Tobar Pharaic, from a well that never runs dry. But occasionally, the cows horns were crooked.

Nowadays, every kitchen is fitted with an electric or gas cooker, a wok and, more recently, a microwave. They help to cook and present food in an edible and attractive way. My mother or any mother of her time, had an open fire, some saucepans, an oven, some pots and a pan. The open fire blazed on the hearth and had to be fed with turf or wood to keep it going. For example, you couldn't put on a cake and go out for a walk. No sir. You had to keep the heat of the fire even, and had to turn the cake and watch it. Nevertheless, I can safely say that a roast stuffed goose done in the oven, with coals over and coals under, was much tastier and more mouthwarming than one done in a cooker today. There was the oven hanging from the hanger, directly over the red hot fire and there were the saucepans all around the hearth, and hey presto, dinner cooked to perfection, potatoes laughing in their jackets, meat smothered in gravy and served on time. How did our mothers do it? And I wonder what would they think of our kitchens today.

To make life easier, I have a washing machine and a tumble drier. I put in the powder, set the programme, hit the button and away it goes. And away I go too. I can go for a walk, or prepare a meal or hang on the telephone, or go shopping or read a book - oh! the list is endless. When the clothes are washed, I can dry them in the tumble drier or hang them on the line. I don't even have to wet my hands.

What a change since my childhood days. Washday meant that preparations began hours beforehand. Water was boiled in large quantities in the pot, the kettle and the saucepans. The large wooden or enamel tub was set on a chair in the middle of the floor, or in the summer, outside in the street. It was filled with boiling water and the washboard was set in it. The very dirty clothes would be steeping since the night before. Then the clothes were washed, scrubbed on the washing board with sunlight soap and, when clean, were squeezed dry. Each item was washed separately, except small items like hankies or socks. The water was changed after every few items, and fresh clean boiling water was used, which meant that an eye had to be kept on the fire, and the pots and the kettle and the clock - as the dinner or lunchtime crept closer. When all the washing was done, clothes were rinsed well in cold water, and then hung out on the line to dry. I remember looking at the line of clean freshly washed clothes - billowing, fluttering, flapping and dancing in the breeze - as if each shirt or each dress had a life of its own, but it never ever dawned on me to assess the immense amount of work attached to any one washday. What suffering, and indeed some mothers suffered more than others, as their families were very numerous indeed. And there we were, spotlessly dressed children, never giving a thought to what washday entailed.

When the modern woman wants a cup of tea in the privacy of her kitchen, she fills the electric kettle from the tap and plugs it in. In five minutes, the kettle boils and she can have her cuppa. In my growing-up-days, when a housewife needed a cup of tea, she went to the tank or maybe to the well for fresh water. She half filled the kettle, and hung it up on the hanger making sure that the fire was roaring up the chimney. Then she waited - and waiting was something the women were very good at - and waited and waited.

Depending on the type of kettle and on the amount of water, it could take half an hour to boil. Then, and only then, could she have her cup of tea, always assuming that she had enough of tea, sugar and milk in the larder. The shop could be three miles away and if there was a baby in the house, the woman was tied and housebound - so no tea.

Nowadays, life would be unthinkable without the fridge. It keeps things fresh and hygienically edible. There were no fridges in our house or in any house in the village. Yet they devised their own methods of preserving food. When the weather was very warm, during those long hot summers, a huge black and cream crock - every house boasted one - was filled with cool, clear, cold water. The milk was poured into a can or bucket and placed into the crock and covered with a piece of muslin or clean white cloth. The water in the crock could be changed as soon as it got tepid or lukewarm - depending on the great heat of the day. In the same way, the butter was put on a dish and left into a basin of cold water, result, no runny butter. In our house, when cairigín or jelly was made, it was put in a glass bowl in the coolness of the parlour and covered. I'm very much afraid that very often this strategy did little to lengthen its life span - if and when we got our spoons into it.

Ironing nowadays is a matter of plugging in an iron, setting a programme and getting the ironing board ready. Plug in the kettle for a cuppa, switch on the radio and sit up on your ironing stool, and off you go. Ironing is very definitely an easy chore. In my youth, it was not so. First of all a huge fire was necessary. An ironing block was stuck into the heart of the fire. The kitchen table was prepared – covered with a small blanket and then a white sheet or a white flour bag scrubbed to death, usually. When the block was really red hot – and this could take 15 minutes – it was taken out and put into the iron-holder and placed on a stand. Then the ironing was done. However, the inside block cooled quickly and had to be re-heated; again more waiting and, at times, ironing could last for hours. Sometimes, a family had two ironing blocks, which made ironing much easier with less waiting as one block was used, while one was heating.

Toast for breakfast is ready in a matter of minutes, in the modern day world. The piece of loaf, already sliced, is put into the toaster, gadget pressed down, and in seconds, up pops the toast, beautifully brown on both sides. Two slices can be done together and indeed a four-slice toaster is a very ordinary appliance nowadays. To toast or not to toast? That was the question in my young days. The main ingredient was a loaf of bread - and in many homes that was a luxury. Brown home-made bread was the norm. So the grinder of bread, unsliced, would be cut into wide canndaí or slices, and impaled on a fork. This fork was held in front of the fire - red coals were the best - black sods were hopeless. When one side was nice and brown, the slice was turned. At the same time, whoever held the fork, ran the risk of getting the face and hands scorched, as well as the toast. But I remember the toast was very well worth waiting for, as, dripping with golden country butter, we munched and chewed our way through each slice, as if it were manna from Heaven.

In my youth, bathrooms were very definitely a thing of the future. We were washed and scrubbed in the big wooden tub in front of the fire - the shades fully drawn - no chance for a "peeping Tom". Going to the toilet presented no problem.. You used the lovely flowery "po" ever ready under the bed at night if you happened to get taken "short". During the day, you locked yourself into the shed at the bottom of the garden, with the huge upside-down bucket and the deep hole in the ground. And, sometimes, just anywhere would do - as Willie Shaughnessy once told the lone tourist who arrived on a bicycle and looking most uncomfortable and crossing and uncrossing his legs, asked "Where is the toilet around here?" Willie just smiled and said, "You have a wide choice, but mind you watch the wind". "Yes", said the tourist, "But where is it?" and Willie happily answered "Gach áit ó seo go cladach, a mac", - Every place from here to the shore!!

So, sitting reminiscing in my modern kitchen, I hope I am a better person just because I have known the two worlds - the hard times and the good times.

Before, during and after

While we were going to local dances, my father was easy enough to handle. But when we began to move exploringly outside Geata Bán, his whole attitude changed. He was under the mistaken impression that all the men in the great, big, wide world were out there waiting to pounce on his quartet of defenceless girls. He needn't have worried one iota! It was no use arguing with him because, like most older people of that time, once he got an idea into his "ceann", it was very difficult either to shift it or even change it. So, my father's reluctance to give us permission to go off dancing remained a stumbling block which, when we failed to dislodge it, we jumped over. Our strategies to do so were devious and, in hindsight, laughable. Suffice it to say that we got going to the dances - either by hook or by crook.

Dancing was the main attraction during those early eventful years. It was in the dancehall in those days that you met your "fate", made eyes at the fellas, flirted with the next door neighbour's son and generally "come hithered" anyone who was willing to look your way. Johnston's Hall in Kinvara ran some great hops. There was a small stage at the far end on which sat the band. Because the hall was not too big, there was only need for one or two microphones. Admission was one shilling for an hour. This was known as the shilling hop and then later on, half a crown for the night. Like all dancehalls at that time, it was always packed to capacity - they came from Duras, Ballindereen, New Quay, Ardrahan and, sometimes, a crowd came from the band's home town.

The structure of the hall was such that the women had to walk right through the hall to get to the clockroom -

and the male population standing around had a good gawk and plenty of time to vet them. There were lots of old time waltzes, half-sets, and Sieges of Ennis. Tap-ins were the vogue at the time - somebody asked you to dance, and before you had done even one lap around the hall, another man tapped you in and took over. Shortly afterwards, another fellow tapped and once more you changed partners. This tap-in business often led to rows and once I saw a fellow refusing to let the girl go and he got a slap in the jaw for his trouble. The bands were usually local ones - Gannons from Loughrea, The Oranmore Ceili Band, Al and Phonsie O'Dea's band from Tuam and Jack Donohue's band from Tynagh. Once, Din Joe, of radio fame, came and performed there and such a crowd came to see him that Ritchie Johnston, the proprietor, had to refuse admission to some of them. So, inside was a huge crowd, cheek to cheek, knee to knee, shoving and pushing and straining to hear and outside was an equally big crowd eager to be entertained. Some smart alec from Ballindereen, either Brendan Jordan or Michael Walshe, pulled off his jacket, threw it on the ground and began to step dance on it. Immediately a crowd formed around him, and he let a few ear splitting yells and whirled around and the crowd cheered and Din Joe was forgotten. A fickle lot they were.

Still, it was Labane Hall which had a certain lure, something which once more proves "that the hills far away are green". Certainly, St. Michael's Hall in Craughwell was a dancing mecca around that time, but it was to Labane we all flocked. Occasionally, I sit and think of all the devious tricks we had to employ to get going to a dance or a date and I wonder are young people any happier nowadays, when things are made so much easier than they were for us. We lived in Duras and had to cycle all the way to Labane – a journey of 8 miles. Did that worry us? Not a whit!

It was an exciting event on a Sunday evening when we met at the Cross of Nogra – fifteen or sixteen of us – all neighbours' children. We loitered for a few minutes and then the pack moved off. They came from all over the parish – Mattie and Paraic Quinn, Alf, Helena and Bernie Mahon, Pat, Mickey and Kate Keane, Michael Mahon,

Tom Bohannon, Bridie, Paddy, Michael and Colie
Linnane, Paddy, Teresa and Kathleen Carty, Martin
Mooney, Delia, Teresa, Peggy and Mattie Hynes, Jimmy
Connors, Paddy, Maureen and Mattie Glynn, Mattie,
Miko and James Fahy, Tommy, Willie and Frank
Kavanagh and us four girls. Needless to say, all of us
didn't always go together but 75% of us did. We
whooshed off up the road, turned left at Geata Bán, down
through the town of Kinvara. The locals there eyed us
with suspicion - in from the country, don't you know! -
and out the Ardrahan road as if all the devils in hell were
after us.

While the weather was fine our journeys to and from
the dancehalls didn't provide many problems, but when
the wintery weather began we suffered then, especially on
windy nights. One such windy night I was finding it very
difficult to cycle up a hill when two of the lads cycled out
of the pack, caught my arms and propelled me forward
effortlessly and soon I was freewheeling down the other
side. The motto was very definitely "all for one, and one
for all". A windy night we could puff against. A frosty
night we could slide and slip against. But we had no
protection against wet weather; it usually spelled disaster.
If we got drenched going to the dance, who on earth
would want to dance with a "lipín báite". So, you can
imagine how discouraged we were until Bal Mahon came
along with his lorry. He pulled up, let down the back flap,
and we all climbed cheerfully on board. We sat together
in the back, huddled closely, absolutely happy. What a
carefree, happy, easily pleased crowd of young people we
were. So on then to the dance, smiles set and expectations
high.

By now everybody knows what used to happen inside
in the dancehall in those good old days. There was an
imaginery line down the middle of the hall which
separated "them" from "them". Men stood on one side,
women stood on the other. There they lounged, eyeing
the females just like you'd see a farmer eyeing cattle at a
fair, and opposite stood the women, passively submitting
to the scrutiny, anxiously waiting for the male to make an
approach. The band struck up and there was a stampede;
the men surged forward and grabbed the women they had

earmarked. Some times a charming chap asked a doting hopeful to dance, over the heads of the mob. He caught her eye, nodded his head, beckoned to the floor and waited. She would leap up, sidestep the lurching dancers and reach the safety of his arms with a happy sigh. When a dance ended, so did the "togetherness". The man turned on his heel and walked away, while the woman walked away in the opposite direction, back to the wall flowers who were dying for news and threw out a barrage of questions. "Did you shift". "What was he like", "Did he dance close?", "Did he book the next dance?", "Did he ask you for a mineral?", and so the next dance was called and the night wore on.

If things went well and you happened to get a fellow, he might ask you to take a walk. But then you had to run the risk of being accosted by the man with the flash lamp - the local priest, Canon Considine. He sat inside the door and knew everybody, and the minute they began to leave in twos or fours, then he left too. Armed with his torch, he went out after them, flashing the light into corners, beside the gates, behind walls, routing the "neckers". "Is that you, Miss Quinn"", he said to me once while I died a thousand deaths, even though all I was doing was trying to get to know a smasher from Gort. "It is, Father", I said. "Well, I'm very disappointed in you", he said. "Get back into the hall and don't let me see you out here again". My partner in crime and I walked sedately around the corner straight for the door, then turned, dashed down the road and resumed our "business"!!

In case anybody gets the wrong idea, the aforementioned priest was a really nice person. He had attacked this new problem of pairing couples who left the safety of the dance hall in a very straight forward and outgoing way. He viewed these walks as a proximate occasion of sin and thought that if he could disturb the tete a tete, he'd avoid lots of trouble. Nobody ever took exception to his reprimands or got annoyed when he accosted them.

After the ball was over, we had to cycle all the way home. Again we travelled in packs and had long and laughing discussions about what had happened and what might have happened, and what didn't happen. I do remember that I always felt hungry and I also remember how several times we descended on a few apple trees like a pack of locusts and left the branches bare and naked. We never did any harm, but an apple snatched from an overhanging branch at night tasted twice as nice as one picked in the orchard during the day.

Having the proper footwear was very important, especially if you wanted to go to the dance in Seapoint, the ballroom in Galway. Once a very memorable incident happened. During the summer holidays, a young clerical student, Martin O'Grady, said he'd "love to go to the dance with us". We were delighted and honoured to have him. Off we went. As we handed in our tickets at the door, we had to show the soles of our shoes to the doorman, "I'm sorry", said the small, cheeky, but very firm, ticket collector, "He cannot go in 'cos he has studs in the soles of his shoes". We looked and, of course, he had; how was it that we had never noticed that before? "There is no use begging", said your man, "Away ye go and don't come back until he gets new shoes". New shoes at nine o'clock at night! We didn't know whether to laugh or to cry. But we weren't beaten yet, even though we had only half a crown between us. We traipsed across the road and began to knock at doors. "Excuse me, would you have such a thing as a pincers please?", "Janey Mack! a pincers, cripes what will ye want next?" We knocked at four doors and struck luck at the fifth. A wizened and whiskery old man with rimless glasses perched on the edge of a button nose said, "I might have now. What do ye want it for?" So we told him and he thought it very funny, but decided to help us on one condition - could he keep the studs and protectors for himself? At that moment in time, we'd have promised him anything and were only too pleased to fulfil any condition. So, out of a rickety old drawer he pulled the pincers and with great precision and dexterity proceeded to denude the shoe soles of studs and protectors. He placed them carefully in the drawer and then handed back the shoes to Martin admonishing him, "Off you go now, and show a clean pair of soles to the doorman", and he closed the door on us, while we were still thanking him. That was a great night and we literally danced the soles off our shoes. In later years Martin

NOT A WORD OF A LIE

became a priest and often laughed when we talked about that episode. "Just imagine us running around Salthill", he used to say, "looking for a pincers. It's a wonder that they didn't have us all certified!".

Weren't the dances great? Weren't the lads we met great? Indeed, wasn't life great? All we cared about was to get to the dance and dance enough, no drugs, no drink, no problems. God be with the old days.

Freedom

For me, Geata Bán was the gateway to the beckoning world. It conjured up all kinds of visions, ideas and notions of what lay beyond. Inside were spread the small community and scattered villages of Duras, while outside stretched the vast expanse of the whole wide world. Inside were limited and boring experiences and the humdrum familiarity of the locality. Outside were adventure, fun, people, new experiences and, above all places, far away places, tantalising and mysterious with strange sounding names. I longed with all my youthful heart to get outside and conquer the world.

Geata Bán, meaning white gate, was the spot where our poor dusty second class road met the main classy tarred highway running from Galway to Clare, or if you prefer from Clare to Galway. It formed a T-shaped junction, our road being the leg while the two arms were flung wide, to stretch endlessly in both directions, appearing to embrace land and sky. Once you were inside and headed for Nogra, nothing new would ever happen. While outside on either road, anything strange and wonderful was liable to occur and the whole world was one's oyster. When we were young, we were never allowed to go next or near the spot, particularly after dark. It was viewed by some as an occasion of sin, and an immediate occasion as well. Anything bad that happened always seemed to happen "up around Geata Bán". It was the pivot around which the whole world revolved, or so we in our limited knowledge believed.

To break free from strict parental supervision long enough to get as far as this forbidden spot was indeed a difficult feat. But once or twice I managed to kick the

153

traces and enjoyed the experience. Once, I ran to Nogra for a message rather late in the evening. My mother had gone to visit her two friends, two returned yanks, Mary Watson and Jane Reidy. My father was engrossed in the Irish Press and I was suddenly free. I raced to the cross of Nogra and confided my intentions to Mary Carty and off we ran. We at last stood at the crossroads and only one lone cyclist could be seen fading into the distance. We walked around and looked longingly, wondering what lay beyond the turns in the road. We lay on the road and put our ears to the ground and in this way could hear a car approaching from four to five miles away. As cars were scarce, and few and far between, lying on the road presented no danger whatsoever. This time we were lucky. We could hear a car coming from afar and we jumped up and ran to safety. We watched as the headlights brought a glow to the sky over around the parish chapel, then on to the turn of Gort Sean Bhó. At this point the glow of the lights almost disappeared as the car approached Cahernamadra Cross. But then, suddenly, they pierced the sky like two great eyes shining as the car came into view and around the turn of Tor Trom.

Mary and I backed off and ran down to the safety of our own road, as the car thundered nearer and nearer. Expecting it to continue on towards Clare, we nearly fainted when it turned in towards us, and halted right beside us. It was good old 6054, belonging to Paddy Gardiner, who had been all over the world and came back to live in Duras. He stuck his head out the window and said, "Are ye coming or going?" We said "coming". "Well, sit in", he said, "and I'll drive ye home". And that's exactly what he did and we were more convinced than ever that marvellous things did happen around Geata Bán. Look at what happened to us! We were being driven home in style by none other than the yank.

Two years later, my second dash to freedom occured. It was bonfire night and, as usual, our family had its own small fire in the boreen opposite our cabbage garden. Only the four girls stood around it, feeding it with brosna or sticks collected the evening before. Mary was encouraged to play the violin and the others pranced around making lots of noise. My parents thought that the best thing for us, was to cocoon us in this sort of protected and isolated atmosphere. I, however, had different ideas and decided that it was time to have a look at another bonfire. So I asked my sisters to talk loudly and to mention my name distinctly whenever my mother appeared at the half door to see how we were getting on. "Please don't go", my sister, Nora, said, "you'll only get into trouble". But I was all keyed up and left, racing past our gate, climbing Sullivan's hill, simply darting past the Mount, in case I saw a ghost, and finally arriving at the cross. There the bonfire was in full swing. All the locals were standing around, some smoking pipes, some Woodbines and one or two chewing bribs of grass. The children were playing hide and seek, and blind-man's-buff, while the older ones roared and threatened them to keep away from the fire. All in all, I was very disappointed and said so to my friend, Delia Hynes, who immediately suggested, "Let's go to Geata Bán. There will be music there". No sooner said than done, and we coaxed Mattie Glynn to come with us and away we ran. Going up around Kavanaghs we heard the music and the laughter and quickened our steps. We thought we'd never be there.

We arrived and I'll never forget my first sight of that bonfire. It was huge and sparks rose high and flames lit up the whole place. The heat was intense, and they kept throwing on sticks and old bicycle tyres and papers. Out on the tarred road, the dancers were dancing a half set to music played by Mattie Quinn as he sat on a gap in the wall. The sound of the melodeon was carried on the breeze, and people were arriving all the time. All the Kavanaghs were there and so were all the Corlesses. Down across the fields, the Hanlons had come and a crowd came from Currenrue. They were singing, and dancing and laughing, all the ordinary things, but for me and my friends, they were touched with magic. Standing at the edge of the group, I looked through the smoke and the sparks and thought, "this is what's on offer in the outside world, this and myriads of similar experiences". Suddenly, it was time to go home and face the music there.

As the noise receded, and the thumping of my heart steadied and the silence of the night once more descended, neither of the three of us was too happy. We had just taken a big step towards adult life. Our childhood was over and we weren't quite sure whether the night had proved as satisfying as we had hoped. For my part, I had jumped the traces and thereby had changed the pattern of things. That which had moulded me was changing and, undoubtedly, I was changing too. My childhood had almost ended and I was on the threshold of the great big beautiful world, the delights of which, up until now, I had only guessed at but which I was soon to sample. And I couldn't wait to get out.